EUDOKIMA EDITIONS

I0540659

Happiness Now!

A GUIDED JOURNEY

UNLEASH MOTIVATION AND TAKE ACTION TO EXPERIENCE GREATER PEACE, MEANING AND JOY

SONIA WEYERS

Copyright © 2017, © 2022 Eudokima

Professionally edited by Katie Chambers
Formatting by Wild Words Formatting
Cover design by Matthieu Touvet

All rights reserved. No part of this publication may be reproduced, distributed, or transmitted in any form or by any means, including photocopying, recording, or other electronic or mechanical methods, without the prior written permission of the publisher, except in the case of brief quotations embodied in reviews and certain other non-commercial uses permitted by copyright law.

WHAT READERS ARE SAYING:

"In *Happiness Now! A Guided Journey*, **DR. WEYERS MASTERFULLY GUIDES THE READER** through a comprehensive exploration of the determinants of happiness, including a thorough look at how to sustain changes in our habits and a menu of 23 activities to choose from. If you're ready to experience a level of happiness you may not even know is possible, **I HIGHLY RECOMMEND THIS BOOK!**"

—Hal Elrod, #1 bestselling author,
The Miracle Morning

***

"Self-help books these days seem to be all the same, but this book is original in all that it encompasses and the calming, guiding tone from the author. You can tell **THE AUTHOR GENUINELY CARES** as she expertly leads you through various areas of focus. While I have heard some of the advice before, Sonia presents it in such a way that makes me actually want to take action."

***

"Amongst the trillion self-help books that exist, this book stands out for its clear and handy program to a happier life. A true guided journey to a happy place, accessible to all! **A LIFE CHANGER...**"

***

"Wow! **WHAT A HELPFUL AND INSIGHTFUL BOOK!** As a life/career coach with decades of experience, I found some new tidbits and exercises that I plan to use with my own clients. Dr Weyers has done a masterful job of combining concepts, advice from others and simple exercises to put together an easy-to-read and inspiring book on making changes in one's life. This definitely stands out in the growing library of personal development books currently on the market, and I plan to recommend it to many of my friends and clients looking for a motivational read!"

* * *

"I found this book both enjoyable and encouraging. Many books are written on the subject of happiness. I think this author steps up to the challenge of offering something fresh and nails it. She presents information that most of us already know in a pleasant way that begs us to just do it already. **I GIVE IT 5+ STARS.**"

* * *

"In this self-improvement book, the author guides the reader by addressing the steps to help make us happier. It's easy for us all to get lost with feelings of unhappiness, but anyone can be unhappy. It's finding the way to choose to be happier and using self-control to create a better life for yourself. This Is **ONE OF THE BEST SELF-HELP BOOKS I'VE READ IN A LONG TIME.** I'll be rereading this often."

DEDICATION

I dedicate this book to my children:

Clara, Gabrielle, Oscar, and Stella.

You are my drivers for bettering myself.
My deepest wish is that you have learned
from me that life offers endless discoveries,
and that you can follow your dreams.

"If you want to awaken all of humanity,
then awaken all of yourself.
If you want to eliminate the suffering
in the world, then eliminate all that
is dark and negative in yourself.
Truly, the greatest gift you have to give
is that of your own self-transformation."

– Lao-Tzu

FREE DOWNLOAD

To thank you for checking out my book, I would like to give you the PDF of the activity booklet I have created as a companion guide. I know that to get the most benefit from the book, putting the suggestions into action is key. People who have used the activity booklet have made much more progress on the path towards Their TRUE Happiness and you can too!

To claim your free gift, simply visit:

https://eudokima.com/happiness-now-guide

Keep the activity booklet close to the book and anytime I ask you to reflect on a question, you will find a place in this booklet to note your thoughts and reflections. I hope you enjoy the journey!

TABLE OF CONTENTS

DISCLAIMER

This book is presented to you for informational purposes and is not a substitute for any professional advice. It is the reader's sole responsibility to seek professional advice before taking any action on their part. Some issues require more expert intervention than simply reading a book. Depending on the nature of the issue, it may be more appropriate to seek help from a professional.

FOREWORD

Two of the most popular questions today are "What is happiness?" and "How do I get more?" Everyone in the industrial world thinks that happiness will come with the next job or the next new car or the next house. But they need to rethink that assumption. A new consumer item may make you temporarily very happy but research shows that, in the not-so-long term, it does not bring most people the kind of happiness they crave. True happiness comes from ongoing positive relationships and positive experiences. Here is some of the latest research about happiness.

According to an article in *Fast Company*, "Research over the last decade or so has sent out a resounding message: If you want to be happier, invest in experiences rather than things. In their groundbreaking work, psychologists Leaf Van Boven and Thomas Gilovich conducted a series of surveys and found that experiences made people happier than goods. Their findings were summarized in the Journal of Personality and Social Psychology." Then in 2010, Gilovich, a professor of psychology at Cornell University, showed why.

Gilovich's study found that when people buy things, they are more likely to suffer buyer's remorse. They also tend to compare their material assets with those of others. On the other hand, it's more difficult to compare other people's experiences with your own. http://psych.colorado.edu/~vanboven/research/ publications/vb_gilo_2003.pdf

Additional research shows that the richer we get, the less happy we become. According to an article on Market Watch by Catey Hill, "A study, published this month in the journal Nature Human Behavior, found that once we reach a certain household income— $105,000 in the United States, $95,000 globally—more income "tended to be associated with reduced life satisfaction and a lower level of well-being." https://www.marketwatch.com/story/the-dark-reasons-so-many-rich-people-are-miserable-human-beings-2018-02-22

In February 2019, *The New York Times Magazine* ran an article entitled "Wealthy, Successful and Miserable." I think the headline says it all. Written by a Harvard alumna at her 15th reunion, she says she was shocked to learn "how many of my former classmates weren't

overjoyed by their professional lives—in fact, they were miserable."
https://www.nytimes.com/interactive/2019/02/21/ magazine/elite-professionals-jobs-happiness.html.

Money, power, and what looks like success, do not always lead to happiness. We need to be careful in our assessment of what brings happiness. In the documentary *Three Identical Strangers,* the identical triplets were separated at birth and purposely put into three different socio-economic homes. One was in a poor home, the second in a middle-class home and the third in a well-to-do-home. When they met years later by accident, it was not surprising how much they looked alike, but what was surprising was that they behaved alike, had the same likes and dislikes and the same expressions. What was the impact of nature vs. nurture? They were identical in all aspects but one: happiness. The triplet with the most loving parents, in this case the lowest income parents, was the one who was the happiest. The unhappiest was the one from the wealthy family who had a less loving and less nurturing childhood. One conclusion you might draw is that income level did not determine happiness; see the film for the complete explanation, Sadly, the triplet from the wealthy home had a very sad outcome: he later committed suicide.

Back to the real world where I lived in Geneva, Switzerland, from 1973 to 1974. It was a happy time for us. Anne had just been born and we were living out on a large farm with cows everywhere. Eventually we moved to the center of Geneva, where the kids went to the UN International School. That is where I met Sonia and her parents. I have known the author, Sonia Weyers, since that time, when she was a five year old girl, who became a close friend of my daughter Susan. I got to know Sonia, a precocious but serious little girl who loved adventure. Even back then she spoke perfect English and perfect French—at the age of five. We kept in touch over the years, spent multiple summers together, and still know each other today after many babies and life experiences. During that forty-five year period, I have seen Sonia go from what appeared to be a happy child to a stressed college student to a very unhappy wife, mother and parent and then reverse all of that misery and become a very happy person in the last ten to twelve years. How did she do that? That is the question we all want to know the answer to because much of the world is not happy no matter their living situation or their material wealth. Happiness seems to be elusive. However, this book gets at the heart of what makes happiness across cultures. It is not just for Western culture; it is for all people. A lot of the lessons that she shares with you are based on her own life experience. She shows how she went from being totally miserable to being very happy, not for just a short time, but all the time. The question is how did she do it? Fortunately, she breaks it down into manageable steps for all of us. Her happiness has endured for years and now she is helping other people achieve happiness in their lives. We can all do it. We just need the right mindset.

The first part of Sonia's book is focused on creating the mindset for happiness, which is the most important part. You can't be happy if you have a negative mindset. She goes into this in great detail. The second part of her book is focused on taking care of yourself. It is hard to be happy if you are physically miserable, emotionally distraught, socially isolated or lacking meaning. These four areas are covered in the second part of the book. In the third part, there are 23 easy steps that you can use, but they have to be practiced. *That is the key*. Nothing happens in life without practice.

These are suggestions on how to take care of yourself, how to take control of your life—you are the one in charge, not your parents, not your spouse, not your coworkers, not your children—YOU! Blaming people only makes you miserable and being angry only makes it worse. Turns out that holding on to anger is like holding onto a piece of hot coal. You are the one who gets burned, according to a quote from Buddha. Happiness is within you as Weyers points out in in the first part of her book. *Happiness is a state of mind*, a decision you make and are responsible for just as Weyers says, and that state of mind is not dependent on material goods. It is a way of looking at the world. It is a state of mind in which gratitude and love of the small things in life play an important role. It comes when people feel like they are part of a community or a team, when they feel respected and trusted and where love and acceptance are part of the culture.

People who live in the blue zones, places with the longest lifespans in the world, have one commonality: they have a supportive sense of community. Here is an Atlantic Monthly article about blue zones.
https://www.theatlantic.com/health/archive/2017/10/get-rid-of-everything/543384/

According to the author of *The Self-Aware Parent*, Fran Walfish, "The deepest pleasures are derived from interpersonal love, warm relationships, giving, appreciation, and gratitude." I couldn't agree more, especially having been a teacher for more than forty years. Children are happiest when they feel love in the classroom; couples are happiest when they feel loved and respected (no surprise here); friends and employees are happiest when they are respected and appreciated for their effort (again no surprise).

SONIA WEYERS

Sonia has searched long and hard for how to be happier, not just for herself, but for her friends, family and children, and she has compiled the lessons she has learned in this book. You will love yourself forever for having read and implemented the suggestions in this book and so will your family and friends. It takes only a couple of hours to read and a few more hours to practice—out of an 80 year life span, that is a tiny amount of time to devote to yourself. You can do it and you are worth it! I applaud her for her passionate goal to make the world a happier place.

Esther Wojcicki
Founder of Palo Alto Media Arts Program
author of *"Moonshots in Education:*
Launching Blended Learning in the Classroom"
and *"How to Raise Successful People:*
Simple Lessons for Radical Results"
March 2019

INTRODUCTION

Are you wanting more out of life? Do you wish that you could feel more peaceful? Are you yearning for more meaning? Are you struggling with negative emotions and looking for more joy? Are you wondering what all this is about?

You are not alone! In this world where material goods have become so easy to desire and acquire, more and more people are looking for peace, for meaning, for joy, for a greater purpose, for a life well-lived.

This book gives you a grounded, no-nonsense approach to examine what is lacking in *YOUR* life and how *YOU* can take action to change that. As a therapist, coach, Your Happiness Guide and the leader of several programs to help my clients to Experience Their TRUE Happiness, already, I have helped many people just like you over the last 15 years find a better quality of life.

The reflections, exercises, and calls to action in this book have already helped busy professionals, stay-at-home parents, and many others create a better quality of life. A participant in one of the workshops related to this book said, "Sonia's workshop gave me great insight into how I could spontaneously spark positive emotions on a minute-to-minute or day-to-day basis that made a genuine difference in my way of interacting with my 'self' and others in my life."

I guarantee that if you read this book, do the exercises, and pick at least one action step to durably incorporate into your life, you will feel improvement in *your* quality of life.

This is not a one-size-fits-all approach; on the contrary, it could not be more personalized. I will lead you to reflect on a variety of topics, and it will be up to *you* to make some choices about what you do and do not want to incorporate in your life.

Don't be the person who complains about their life and then does nothing about it; don't be the person who passes up an opportunity to take positive action for their life.

Be the kind of person who integrates positive change in their life. Be the kind of person who inspires others with their positive changes. Be the kind of person who takes charge of their life *now*.

The life-satisfaction-boosting tips you will find in each chapter are all tried and tested, and most of them are backed by science. To reap some of the benefits for *your* life, all you need to do is follow the invitations, and you'll create a life that you once only dreamed of.

In this book you'll be able to:

1. Craft some routines

2. Clarify your sleep needs

3. Reflect on your social needs

4. Make some choices about food

5. Make some choices about exercise

6. Experience gratefulness

7. Experience self-compassion

8. Experience forgiveness

9. Visualize your ideal life

This book will take you on a journey of personal growth as you explore your views on different important areas of your life. You may find that it stretches you in places, and you may even experience some discomfort; however, I promise you that if you follow through and take action where prompted, you will find yourself on the way to creating a life more true to your core and experiencing a sense of self-realization.

If you find that you struggle to implement the changes, I have included ways in which you can work with me further. So, know that I've got your back and get on the way to finally finding and experiencing Your TRUE Happiness.

There is one caveat: while a good life obviously includes a professional activity and the balancing of some financial issues, I do not talk about these in this book. Instead, I focus on how to have better experiences in your life, whatever the circumstances, and this really works for most sets of circumstances.

I can promise you these things because I have personally experienced them myself. When I was 20, I was quite unhappy without any externally visible reasons, stressed out a lot, and did not exercise. I was blessed with fairly good health but did get regular sinus infections and took antibiotics at least a couple of times most years.

I am now over 50; I am happier than I have ever been, a lot of the time; I know how to manage my stress; I exercise regularly; and I enjoy better health than I have ever had and haven't taken antibiotics for several years now.

For the last three decades, I was on a journey fraught with unhappiness where circumstances didn't seem to warrant that, soul-searching when my path seemed traced for me already, and an unrelenting search for better times. What you will find in the pages that follow is both rooted in my own quest and also validated by scientific studies.

My biggest hope in writing this book is that you will find some insights that expand *your* perspective, some clues that will lead to some positive changes in *your* life and some inspiration to get up and take charge of it. I am inviting you to invest some time and focus to create a better future for *YOU*.

Take your quality of life in your own hands today. Engage in increasing your life satisfaction and start reaping the benefits of creating a life that suits *YOU*.

Enjoy the ride!

The rest of the book is structured in three parts. Part I will focus on cultivating your mindset to help prepare you to receive maximum benefits from the explorations that follow.

In Part II, you will look at different areas of focus, in which you will discover levers for increasing your well-being. You will look at your Health, both Physical and Emotional, Relationships, and Spirituality and Meaning.

In Part III, to help you incorporate these principles into your daily life, you will focus on action steps: 23 activities to help enrich the various areas of focus outlined in Part II.

Editorial note: to avoid cumbersome he/she, his/her and the like, whenever the gender can be either masculine or feminine, I will arbitrarily choose the feminine. This book can be one place for reversed gender bias.

Part 1

MINDSET

In this first part, I invite you to stroll with me through the garden of the various flowers that constitute the great mindset needed to pursue your goals. In Part II, you will go deep into the four areas of focus for increasing your wellbeing, and in Part III, you will learn a selection of activities that can make an amazing difference in your life.

For Part I, Chapter 1 is about Motivation; Chapter 2 is about Commitment; Chapter 3 is about Beliefs; Chapter 4 is about Perseverance; and Chapter 5 brings it all together to create your future, in which you will be empowered to Cultivate *Your* TRUE Happiness.

"Every journey, no matter how great,
begins with a single step."
– Lao Tzu

"Dare to live the life you have
dreamed for yourself.
Go forward and make your
dreams come true."
– Ralph Waldo Emerson

Later in the book, I will invite you to write some things down. I have created a companion PDF Activity Booklet, which you can download for free by going to

https://eudokima.com/happiness-now-guide

Alternatively, you can use a notebook. In that case, I invite you to choose a special notebook that you dedicate to your journey in this book.

Chapter 1

FINDING MOTIVATION

Why?

First, ask yourself, "Why?" Why do you want to embark on this journey? What led you to pick up this book?

The first ingredient of any motivation is the answer to a "Why" question. If you want to start a new behavior or change a habit, you must have a reason for doing it. Is something in your life not working for you? Do you have a pain point? Or do you have an objective? A dream? Something you really want that you do not yet have?

Think about it, when do you ever do anything without a reason?

There can be a variety of reasons! Think of how you spend your days, your weeks. You probably get up every day, go to work or to school or some activity, and do some chores like going grocery shopping for your household or doing the laundry. Now these are what a lot of us might consider obligations. We do them because we have to.

Well, I invite you to think slightly differently, to think of a motivating "why" for those obligations. I do laundry so that I have clean clothes to wear. I shop for food because I need to eat. I work to earn an income that allows me to do things. But even if you consider that there are things you do "because you have to," I encourage you to think about some things that you do by choice.

Take a few moments right now to think of something you do by choice and think of why you do it.

Try to feel how that "why" gives you motivation to do the behavior.

Now take some time to clarify why you are reading this book? It probably has something to do with wanting to live a more satisfying life.

What?

> "Knowing what you want is
> the first step in getting it."
> – Louise Hart

Second, you must ask yourself, "What?" What do you want to get out of reading this book? What is your objective? What are you yearning for that you don't have yet? Take a few moments to dive into that a bit more. What, specifically, do you want to improve in your life?

You might find that your life is bland and you want some excitement. You might wish to feel sadness or anger less often. You might feel lonely even though you are surrounded by people. What is *your* specific reason for reading this book?

Why Now?

Lastly, in determining your motivation, ask yourself, "Why now?" What happened that caused you to pick up this book now? Was there an event that triggered your quest for a stronger well-being, or have you had a lingering feeling for a while? Spend a few moments now to reflect on this.

I appreciate you for taking this step and for taking charge of your well-being, and I invite you to appreciate yourself as well.

Some of you may want to have a measure of how much better your life can get if you follow my lead throughout this book. If this is your case, I suggest that you take Diener's Satisfaction with Life Scale, which you can find by searching on the internet for "Life Satisfaction Scale Questionnaire – Excel at Life." With this questionnaire, you can assess your current well-being, and then you can take it again after about three months of imple-menting some of the changes I suggest in this book. You can also try one of Martin Seligman's tests on his website "Authentic Happiness" at the University of Pennsylvania.

What to Do?

OK, so you have a better idea of why you are reading this book and what you want from it. But, now what? Often, even if you know what you want, you feel lost as you don't know what to do to get what you want.

> "Insanity: doing the same thing over and over again and expecting different results."
> – Albert Einstein

If you want to see a change in your life, you will have to change some behaviors. It really is that simple. If you want nothing to change, keep doing what you're doing. But you are holding this book so I trust that you want something to change.

Let me tell you a bit about my own journey here.

I was quite depressed when I was a young adult, and I had absolutely no clue what to do about it. On the surface, I had everything I needed. I had no material strife, had not been abused, and was doing well in school. I often heard, "You have everything needed to be happy." Let me tell you, this is completely unhelpful when you are NOT happy.

This made it even harder to know what to do. I had everything, and I wasn't happy so I went into therapy. Fast forward 30 years, I spent about half of that time in therapy and searched just about every course, every tool, every approach and can honestly say I have found a level of peace and fulfillment that I never even knew was possible 30 years ago.

I Lead You

This book is not offering therapy, don't get me wrong, although I am actually a therapist, but I do intend to lead you through activities and deep reflections that will allow you to make choices for yourself, to choose some new behaviors, and discover what gives you the effect that you are most looking for.

I cannot emphasize enough that you can read this book all you want, but you will only see the changes you are hoping for if you implement some new behaviors.

Throughout the coming pages, I will suggest things for you to try, TRY THEM! I don't promise that everything works for everyone nor that it will be easy. I do promise, however, that if you don't try anything new, nothing will change.

Doubts

Of course you may have doubts: you might be thinking that this is a scam, another set of worthless promises. You may seriously doubt that it could be that simple.

I am just asking that you please give me a chance. What I am presenting to you in this book is a collection of possibilities that are abundantly verified, some by many scientific studies, and others by their sheer timelessness. I have also personally experimented with everything that I propose to you.

- Request #1: I will make a few requests of you, and the first one is that you withhold judgment until after you have tried what I suggest. I request that you grant me your open-mindedness for the duration of our journey together in this book.

Curiosity

Open-mindedness is rooted in curiosity. Come back to why you are reading this book. What would it be like to have the results that you are longing for; what would that feel like? What might happen if you actually implement some new behaviors?

I invite you to be curious. Be curious what you can find out, curious what resources you can find, inside yourself, that you didn't know existed, and curious how your life could change.

Have you ever met someone and wondered what it would be like to be like them? Well my aim is for you to transform your life so that you can experience being a different version of you.

In the following chapter, you will explore the next ingredient of your mindset, the fuel for it: commitment.

Chapter 2

COMMITMENT

It's important for this journey that you "work" to get to know yourself even better. When I ask you a question, please take time to think about it, close your eyes, and reflect. To begin with, I would like you to think about what commitment is like for you, what your habitual responses are to commitment.

Do you treat commitment as though it has little to no value? Do you commit to something and then just pursue your life as though nothing happened?

Or do you take your commitments more seriously than anything else? Do you put everything else aside to make sure you respect your commitments?

Do you have an easy time with commitments? A hard time?

Can you think of a few examples of commitments you have kept? Can you think of at least two or three?

Now think of how you kept them, whether it was easy or difficult, and the various ways you stayed with your commitments even when it might have been difficult.

Now can you think of a couple of examples where you didn't honor your commitments? Can you remember what happened? Was there an incident that propelled the breach or was it sort of negligence, did it slip your mind, did you not pay proper attention?

Changing your habits is difficult. Habits have become automatic ways of doing things so changing them will require different strategies. In this chapter, I encourage you to broaden your awareness of your own relationship to commitment, just so you know what you are up against.

> "Most people fail,
> not because of lack of desire, but,
> because of lack of commitment."
> – Vince Lombardi

To help you honor your commitments, you have a precious ally, which is willpower. Let's explore a bit how willpower works.

First, how is your willpower? Are you able to will yourself to do things you don't feel like doing in the moment, even though you know that later you will have wished you had done them? Or do you have a hard time completing things that are not appealing in the moment?

If you want a whole book on willpower, I recommend *The Willpower Instinct* by Kelly McGonigal. What I present here is a very condensed version of that. In a nutshell, the ingredients of willpower fall into five different categories.

First, there is the physiology of commitment. All willpower challenges are easier if you:

- sleep enough
- eat healthy
- exercise
- meditate

Ironically, we ordinarily think these things require willpower, when in reality they support our willpower better than most other things.

Can you think of a time when you went out and had too much to eat or to drink, too much sugar, whatever food excess? Perhaps you didn't sleep quite as well as a result and perhaps you couldn't quite motivate yourself to exercise the next morning, or to work on that project you have been wanting to take care of for weeks.

Conversely, imagine you just had a fun evening with a reasonable amount of healthy foods; you had a good, restful night; and you woke up eager to go for a run and make progress on your goals.

This should convince you that there is such a thing as the physiology of willpower, so you should use what willpower you do have to focus on sleeping enough, eating healthy, exercising, and meditating as those in turn will help further your willpower for everything else. I will come back to that in Part II.

The second thing you can do to promote your willpower is to be kind to yourself if and when you fail. Self-compassion helps with willpower. I will talk more about self-compassion in Chapter 7 but for now, just remember that you will be more successful if you are kind to yourself when you fail.

The third ingredient of willpower is visualizing your future self. This helps you realize that future-you is connected to present-you and will make you care more about what happens to that person.

The fourth element of willpower is that thinking about the ways in which you might fail and planning how you will recover is more effective for willpower than tracking your success.

A number of studies show that when people are reminded of their success and take note of their progress, they are much more likely to do something inconsistent with their goals. In order to combat that, you want to think about how you might fail. To do this, you can use defensive pessimism, which is a strategic use of pessimism to help you stay on track. It works by answering the following questions:

1. What is my goal?

2. What would be the most positive outcome?

3. What action will I take to reach this goal?

4. What is the biggest obstacle?

5. When and where is this obstacle most likely to occur?

6. What can I do to prevent the obstacle?

7. What specific thing will I do to get back to my goal when this obstacle happens?

The fifth and final element of willpower is the ability to "surf the urge." This means to have the ability to tolerate discomfort when you are tempted to stray from your goals. One example of surfing the urge is to hold your breath just a little longer than what is comfortable. The ability to hold your breath for 15 seconds, even though you may have the urge to breathe, is actually linked to your ability to follow through on your goals.

Now, to summarize willpower rules:

1. Train your willpower physiology (meditating, sleeping, exercising, healthy diet).

2. Forgive yourself (next time you have a willpower setback).

3. Make friends with your future-self (think about the future in a way that feels real)

4. Predict your failures (even if it's really nice to imagine success, be interested in how you might fail) and plan your response.

5. Surf the urge (when you are facing temptation).

So there are things you can do to promote your willpower. It remains that when you commit to something, the first person you are committing to is yourself. Unfortunately, your mind has a way of arranging for things to be okay even when they are not in your best interest.

So it is useful to have an accountability partner. Someone who knows what you are trying to achieve and who is there to keep you honest. That's exactly what I provide for my clients in my program **The "Experience Your TRUE Happiness" Haven.**

It is now time to ask yourself a hard question. Can you commit to trying out what I propose to you in this book? How much time can you commit every day to the pursuit of your own well-being?

Think about that, please!

You are in it for the long run so exploring your commitment is the first step. You must also then think about how to support the commitment so that you really get to the results. I don't want you to put this book on your shelf, not look at it, and not do anything with it; this book is aimed at helping you bring positive and durable changes in your life. But, you must be committed to doing something with it.

- Request #2: Give yourself a real chance.

In the next chapter, you will explore how your beliefs affect your mindset. It is quite possible that your beliefs are holding you back more than you think.

As you work on cultivating the needed mindset to begin your journey, it often helps to collaborate with others. You may want to join the Facebook group "Happiness Now! A Guided Journey."

To join it, just go to www.facebook.com; if you don't yet have an account you will have to create one and then search for the phrase "Happiness Now! A Guided

Journey." You should find the group, click the request to join, and I will be happy to welcome you.

Chapter 3

BELIEFS

Now that you are better able to motivate yourself and commit, you need to explore your beliefs. I am not talking about religious beliefs here, but rather your beliefs about the world, people, and situations. These beliefs are often unconscious or at least not completely conscious.

For example, if no one in your family has attended college for several generations, you just might believe that you don't have what it takes to go to college, and you might not question that belief for even a second, perhaps giving up dreams and aspirations in the process.

Conversely, if your family consists of highly academic people, you might believe that academic success is in your DNA. You might not work hard at all, as DNA-stuff must surely come naturally, and as a result, you might be academically mediocre and end up being the "black sheep of the family." In a similar academic family, your aim might be to become a carpenter, but your implicit belief that you "should" be academically inclined just might derail you, in spite of your passion and competence.

"Your beliefs become your thoughts,
Your thoughts become your words,
Your words become your actions,
Your actions become your habits,
Your habits become your values,
Your values become your destiny."
– Mahatma Gandhi

You have picked up this book with the intention to change your life in some way. You must first ask yourself, do you believe that you can do this? Do you believe there is something you can do to improve your quality of life from the inside? Do you believe, like Mahatma Gandhi, that your destiny stems from your beliefs?

If you have never thought about it, that might seem crazy! It took me a really long time to come to terms with the idea that my beliefs could shape my reality and not the other way around. To some extent, it all starts with a leap of faith. If you are not ready for that, please bear with me for a bit longer.

- Request #3: Suspend judgment for the moment.

In Chapter 1, you looked at your objectives for reading this book. Now I invite you to prepare to think differently about beliefs. If you think about the changes that you want to bring upon your life at this time, what beliefs would support that? Think about that for a moment. I strongly suggest that you include something like "I have what it takes to improve my quality of life."

If you are new to this exercise, it may be easier to think of someone else who already has what you want. What might they believe? Try to put yourself in the shoes of someone who already has made the changes you want in your life.

Take a moment to formulate and write down in this book some of the beliefs that would support the life you dream of:

"Thoughts become things...
Choose the good ones!"
– Mike Dooley

As an illustration to this, I would like you to consider the well-known story of Jim Carrey. He grew up in a very poor family, and even though it seemed likely that he would follow his parents in poverty, Jim always had a lot of hope for his future.

In 1990, Jim Carrey was a struggling young artist trying to make it in Los Angeles. That night, he drove his old beat-up Toyota to the top of a hill. As he sat there, looking over the city, dreaming of his future, broke as he was, he wrote himself a check for $10 million 'for acting services rendered,' and dated it for Thanksgiving 1995. He stuck that check in his wallet—and the rest, as they say, is history. By 1995, Jim had had amazing success and was making up to $20 million per film.

You may be wondering if this is magic, but I assure you it is not. Yet, it sure feels like magic when three ingredients are put together:

1. Purpose: you feel aligned, in agreement with your deepest values, congruent, and confident that you are on the right path.

2. Commitment: you are committed and have put in place a way to honor your commitment.

3. Hard work: you go after your goals; you don't just sit and wait for them to materialize.

You may have heard of the law of attraction. It does not say "sit on your couch, visualize your dreams, and they will appear!" The law of attraction invites you to be really clear on what you want, commit to it, and then orient your life towards it. And then things will start to shift.

If you are more scientifically-minded and find this a little hard to swallow, consider the cognitive biases studied by psychologists. Our human brains process so much information that it uses heuristics to make decisions and this leads to biases. One such heuristic has us looking for evidence that confirms our current view of the world.

This is called the confirmation bias. Basically, we dislike it when our beliefs are in contradiction with the circumstances we are in. As a result, we have a mostly unconscious habit of acknowledging the perspectives that confirm our pre-existing views, while simultaneously ignoring or dismissing opinions—no matter how valid—that threaten our world view.

So when you think that the world is a nasty place and that there is no opportunity anymore in this day and age, you will be drawn to the abundant media coverage of all the tragedies happening all over the planet. When you think that the world is full of opportunity, you can find an equally abundant amount of information on truly inspiring stories of people who took actions that improved the lives of hundreds or thousands of people.

The law of attraction works with that too. Your beliefs will orient your attention and your experience of life. This in turn will change the way you act, based on your expectations. Hence, your experience of life will be different, and it is then easy to see how your beliefs can profoundly impact your life.

I can illustrate this from my own life. I walked around for a long time with a belief that nobody could really love me. It was painful. Every close relationship I had somehow confirmed that belief.

Fast forward a couple of decades of therapy, of learning new ways of thinking and being, and I no longer have this issue in my life. It wasn't easy, and it certainly wasn't quick. I think if I had discovered some of the ideas I share in this book earlier, it might have saved me a lot of time!

A good starting point for shifting your beliefs is to use affirmations. Affirmations are short, powerful statements. They are you being in conscious control of your thoughts. Most of our thoughts are unconscious and research shows that about 80% of our thoughts are negative. Affirmations, then, are your conscious positive thoughts.

Affirmations capture something you wish to include in your life; their job is to support you. We read affirmations to reaffirm what we are committed to, we read affirmations so that our subconscious mind will hear them and—little by little—we incorporate them into our beliefs, and they will support and sustain our mindset.

I recommend that for the moment you choose affirmations that reflect the beliefs you identified above, that support the goals you have for this book. Try to pick two or three affirmations at this point.

- Affirmation 1:

- Affirmation 2:

- Affirmation 3:

One of my affirmations is "I commit to opening myself up to receiving the love that I need." Remember the story I told earlier about believing that no one could love me? I refuse this belief now and put things into place to change it.

It's important when you read an affirmation that you use your imagination so that it feels true. If I read the above affirmation and a little voice in my head goes "Yeah right, like *that's* gonna happen!" then that totally defeats the point. We will come back to affirmations in

Part III when we talk about morning and evening routines.

Now that you have explored the impact of your beliefs on your life and started on the path of consciously choosing your beliefs, you need perseverance, which is the next building block for creating the life that you want.

Chapter 4

PERSEVERANCE

Even when you have motivation, you are committed, and you are working on aligning your beliefs, the going sometimes still gets rough. So the question then is: "How do you keep going when the going gets rough?" The answer: perseverance!

If you have a goal, you probably have a strategy for implementing it. But, you might feel tired and feel like you lack the energy to do your goal-related activity. Other things might come up, which are more exciting, more urgent, more compelling, easier, the list goes on. You might be distracted by the news on TV, by the kids making noise, by the phone ringing. You are vulnerable to all that when you don't prioritize adequately.

Because discouragement WILL strike, it's hard to change your habits, to take on new behaviors. But I'm going to help you find ways to keep going. You need to put systems in place to better deal with these issues, when they come along.

I will start with a somewhat counterintuitive idea, which links to a key insight of the Greek and Roman Stoic philosophers: sometimes the best way to address the uncertainty of your future is to focus, not on the best-case scenario, but on the worst.

According to the Greek and Roman Stoic philosophers, if you feared a certain condition, you should try it on; so for example, if you feared losing your wealth, Seneca would advise that you live as if you were poor, all the while reminding yourself that this is what you feared.

Without going quite to those lengths, defensive pessimism is one of the best ways to prevent yourself from derailing; I detailed defensive pessimism in Chapter 2. It's a great technique for preventing you from giving up.

In order to increase your chances of reaching your goals, think about what might go wrong and then plan what you can put in place now, so that *when* you derail, you can get back on track. For perseverance, much like for willpower, it is also critical that you show self-compassion if you stray from your goal-related path.

I will talk about self-compassion later in the book but just be forewarned. There is abundant scientific evidence to show that beating yourself up is much less effective than showing self-compassion. It's important to stay focused and to forgive yourself for your momentary lapses.

Moreover, it will help you stay the course if you are accountable to more than yourself. Your commitment to yourself is very important. But when the going gets rough, that is the easiest commitment to let go of.

So I strongly encourage you to get a buddy, someone who is either on this journey with you or who is on another journey, so that you can support one another. Then tell people that you are engaged on this path. The more people you tell, the more people will expect you to do it, and that will make you more accountable. You can also follow me on Instagram (@soniaweyers.eudokima) for regular shots of motivation, inspiration and thought-provoking questions.

What do YOU need when the going gets rough? Take some time now and think about how a well-intentioned person could best support you in a way that would motivate you to stay the course.

Your needs:

Don't hesitate to reach out and get support. Find someone in your environment, who is reliable, and tell them what you need from them. You might be surprised to receive exactly the support that you need.

Most of all, to help with perseverance, it's important to remember your "why," to remember your motivation: what you want, why you want this, and why now. If you pick a "why" that matters to you, it just might suffice to motivate you!

The next set of tips may be enough to jumpstart you if you are only mildly derailed or just tempted to derail from your plan.

First, choose an action to improve your mood such as purposefully laughing in front of a mirror or doing a few jumping jacks.

I also suggest using a power song. This is a song that makes you want to move, to dance, to get into motion, one that energizes you. Have it on whatever device you are likely to have around you when your motivation sinks so you can listen to it. If you have chosen it well, it will re-motivate you.

Second, start small. Set a timer for five minutes. Do the behavior that you want to start doing for those five minutes. Chances are you will want to keep going once you have started, but even if you don't, five minutes is a lot better than nothing.

Finally, if you have a role model, think about what *they* would do in your situation and see if you can do the same.

You now should have explored a bunch of different ways to muster some perseverance. What is going to work for you? In the next chapter, I will bring together the elements of a Great Mindset that were covered in the last four chapters. This will send you on the path of exploring your life improvements.

Chapter 5

CREATING YOUR FUTURE

You have now explored your mindset, one ingredient at a time: finding motivation, committing, identifying your beliefs, and finding perseverance. Together they give you the elements of a great mindset.

By developing this mindset, you have found reasons why you are on this journey, you have shed light on your commitment to walking the walk, you have clarified a set of beliefs that support the life you want to create, and you have learned some tools for finding perseverance when the going gets tough.

With all this, you are now ready to go into Part II of this book, which teaches the various areas you can focus on to help you change things. My objective with this book is that you will find ways to become a greater and grander version of you and live a great life.

What that means to you is entirely up to you! I am merely showing you different things to try, and I am one hundred percent convinced that among those you will find a way to significantly improve your quality of life.

I will lead you through exploring your health, both physical and emotional, your relationships in this world, and your spirituality and meaning, how you can connect with a sense of being part of something bigger.

I will cover one area at a time. In each area and sub-area, I will give you some information, and at times, I will invite you to experiment with a specific behavior or reflect on your deep wishes for your life. In each area, you will explore and experiment with different things for you to clarify what YOU want for yourself in this area, in order to live life to its fullest.

After reading Part II, you should have a better idea of which area(s) you want to focus on. In Part III, you can then determine which action steps you will take to help you improve those areas of focus, which will enhance your overall experience of life.

I cannot emphasize enough the importance of actually trying things out. Reading personal development books does NOT develop people. What helps you to evolve is trying on different behaviors and having new experiences. Reading may change the way you think of the world, but no amount of thought will have any impact if it is not followed by some action! Experience is what expands your sense of possibility.

Once you have tried a variety of new behaviors, your mindset will help you decide which behaviors you want to keep, and then you can use the skills you have developed to keep doing the behaviors that support your goals for improving your life.

I strongly recommend, however, that you try one thing at a time and that you do not try adding all the suggestions into your life all at once. Just like a baby starting on solid foods, if you give a baby six new foods at once and she gets a rash, you will not know which food suited her and which one caused the reaction.

If you try to revamp your entire life all at once, you WILL get indigestion! And that is likely to have one and only one consequence: you will quit and go back to the way you were doing things before. That is NOT why you are reading this book; so, pace yourself.

Try the things I suggest, see how you like them, see if you'd like to incorporate them into your life, make a note of which behaviors you would like to incorporate, and then proceed with caution. Don't overdose on well-being, for Heaven's sake!

As you embark on Part II, it is useful to refocus on why you are reading this book in the first place. This is your ultimate motivation, your goal. Write down your goal now. I invite you to look at it every time you pick up this book.

Your Goal:

Having your goal clearly in mind will help you in your exploration. If you are too stressed, you might be particularly interested in contemplative practices that help soothe you. If you are too tired, you might want to focus on your sleep habits. If your diet is not working for you, you might be more interested in exploring eating habits.

Sometimes you might be surprised by the effects of a small change so I recommend that you be open to having unexpected benefits from behavioral changes.

As I will emphasize again as we progress through the different areas, I strongly encourage you to try things at least once or do at least five minutes of a new thing. Start small but become an unrelenting explorer.

As you begin to incorporate new behaviors, you will see changes and others just might notice. One of the best rewards for doing transformational work is when someone else gets inspired and begins to shift her own life.

This book is about using tools to help you cultivate a better well-being, no matter what, regardless of your circumstances. Life will throw curve balls at you, that is a near certainty. But it turns out that feeling bad, feeling anxious, feeling angry etc., never changed anything *out there*, it only makes you more miserable *in here*. In this book, I invite you to develop skills that will allow you to take life in stride, handle the tough times more peacefully, and enjoy the good times more fully.

As I move through the areas of focus, note that your situation may warrant a specialist. You may, for example, need to consult a nutrition specialist or a sleep doctor to help you with your specific needs. With that being said, I offer to you my scientifically-backed recommendations which have helped me and others along our journeys. I can be your happiness specialist ☺!

Before we launch into part II and the areas of focus, I would like to draw your attention to the fact that without a proper mindset, you cannot be open to more happiness, or to any change for that matter.

Being open is the first step to having access to more happiness and it is more subtle than first meets the eye. No one will spontaneously admit to not being open to more happiness and yet it happens more than you think, in insidious ways.

That's why I have created a special meditation to help you to truly open yourself up to the possibility of Your TRUE Happiness. I am offering you this meditation for free, just follow this link:

https://eudokima.com/openness-meditation

Part II

AREAS OF FOCUS

In the first part of this book, you created the mindset needed to start your journey towards improving your life satisfaction. In this second part, you will look at the areas to focus on when aiming for greater peace, meaning, joy, and quality of life.

Quite simply, these areas are your physical health, your emotional health, your relationships, and your spirituality and meaning. This part is an overview of things to consider in these four areas of your life.

As you read this section, please make some notes about what area(s) you feel compelled to work on, and in Part III when I discuss taking action, you will know which action steps are best for you. Also, you may want to conduct your own research in the areas that interest you. While I aim to leave no stone unturned, everyone's journey is different.

Don't leave these areas unexamined or you would run a high risk of living your life on an unfulfilling auto-pilot, a bit like a robot. This is one big obstacle to Your TRUE Happiness! In working with my clients, I have found that there a 5 such obstacles and I have put them into a guide that you can download right here:

https://eudokima.com/5-things

For Part II, Chapter 6 is about Your Physical Health; Chapter 7 is about Your Emotional Health; Chapter 8 is about Relationships; and Chapter 9 is about Spirituality and Meaning.

"An investment in knowledge
pays the best interest."
– Benjamin Franklin

"Knowledge is power.
Information is liberating.
Education is the premise of progress,
in every society, in every family."
– Kofi Annan

Chapter 6

YOUR PHYSICAL HEALTH

"Keeping your body healthy is an expression of gratitude to the whole cosmos – the trees, the clouds, everything."
– Thich Nhat Hanh

"When health is absent, wisdom cannot reveal itself, strength cannot fight, wealth becomes useless, and intelligence cannot be applied."
– Herophilus

"Those who think they have not the
time for bodily exercise will sooner
or later have to find time for illness."
– Edward Stanley

"If anything is sacred,
the human body is sacred."
– Walt Whitman

"The first wealth is health."
– Ralph Waldo Emerson

Nurturing Your Health

Your physical health is the cornerstone of all of your
endeavors; it is of paramount importance. If you are in
poor physical shape, whether you are sick with a
chronic disease, out of shape, or struggling with your
weight, this is likely going to make everything else more
difficult.

Conversely, good health affords you possibilities in life
that you just don't have if you are putting energy and

resources into taking care of a health condition. That much is obvious. What is less obvious is why so many continue to make bad choices for their health even when they understand this principle.

For some, it stems from a lack of information—they don't know how. For others, it can be because of a lack of motivation—they don't really care. For others still, it might be because of a lack of willpower—they can't help themselves.

What is holding *you* back from cultivating excellent health? Is it information? Is it motivation? Is it will-power? The answer to this question can guide you in your search for better health.

As you read, I strongly urge you to think about the different ways in which you can enhance your physical health.

I have been on a personal path for several years to cultivate better health, and I have had very good success. I am over 50, I have four children, and I am physically in the best shape of my life.

The research I have done and the strategies I have put into place are truly working for me, and I invite you to try on whatever parts of that you feel compelled to.

1: Food

My favorite sources for food advice are Dr. Andrew Weil – www.drweil.com – and Isabel De Los Rios – www.beyonddiet.com.

The literature on food, what to eat, what not to eat, the marketing, the diversity of options, the attractiveness of junk food, have all become quite overwhelming if you don't know specifically what you are looking for. Here are a few principles that I have become quite convinced of from my own personal research.

- We really are what we eat: what we put into our body determines to a large extent how our body can function, how well it can extract nourishment for our cells and protect our organs. I encourage you to look at everything you eat for a week and answer one question: Is this the best I can do to take care of my body? If the answer is "no" then start looking at what you can change. I will give you some suggestions below.

- Processed foods are no good: when natural foods are transformed and different chemicals are added for color, taste, and/or appearance, the resulting food bears little resemblance to the original ingredient, and this is not at all innocuous from a nutritional perspective.

Prepared meals are higher in fats, and usually not the healthy fats that we benefit from; they are higher in salt and higher in sugar.

Most commercial snack foods are just junk. Have you ever wondered how they get those so-called potato chips to stack so neatly? Well, it's because they are not made with potato pieces. Potato is merely an ingredient of the process by which evenly shaped chips are made to resemble neatly cut pieces of fried potato. So as I tell my kids, I first advise that when it comes to food:

Eat food that remembers where it came from!

What do I mean by that? I mean eat food that has not gone through too many layers of transformation. I don't mean that butter is a problem because it came from milk but is now in a different form. I mean eat as many single-ingredient foods as possible and prepare your own meals.

You might say that you don't have time to do that. That may be the case, but being ill takes time too. There are ways to save time regarding food. You can make big batches and freeze several meals; make tonight's dinner and tomorrow's lunch at the same time. Eating healthy doesn't necessarily take more time: you can have almonds and an apple for a snack rather than a snack bar and a pack of chips, for example.

- Eat less meat and more vegetables: The evidence concerning how meat impacts your health is somewhat mixed, and I will not take a stand on that. However, the environmental impact of producing meat is not up for debate.

For environmental reasons, I have been focusing on eating less meat, and for health reasons, I have started eating meat from reliable local sources and avoiding industrial meat. More and more people are vegetarian and eating meat has become an increasingly loaded issue. I tread with caution here, but I do warn of the environmental impact, and the water consumption, of the meat industry.

It is also clear that eating lots of fresh fruits and vegetables is better for your health than eating junk food; that much is trivially obvious! The thing to watch, from a health perspective, is to not eat too many pesticides and other harmful chemicals. So to the extent possible, eat fresh, organically grown produce.

In order to do this, you might find it helpful to buy as much as possible from local sources: farmer's markets or other short circuits. This may not be possible or desirable in your particular location, but it is worth looking into.

In Europe, a young organization called "La Ruche Qui Dit Oui" (this translates as "The beehive that Says Yes") puts consumers and local producers (within a 250km/155mi radius in France) in touch through an online platform. There is also Community Supported Agriculture (CSA), where customers purchase a share of a farm's production. When I can't have both, I have personally come to prefer food from short circuits over organic food that has flown half-way across the world to get to me.

Buying food locally does imply accepting more limited options. When living in northern Europe, for example, there are no locally grown bananas or avocados. From my perspective, buying as much local food as possible makes a lot of sense from an environmental, a social, and a health-conscious perspective.

If you take only one thing from this chapter, take this last recommendation.

- <u>Cut out added sugar!</u> This is not going to be easy because it is estimated that sugar is added in roughly

80% of processed food. Also, sugar increases your blood flow to the same areas of the brain as cocaine or heroin; thus, it is highly addictive.

If you are aiming for good health, you better find a way to give up sugar-laden processed foods. Sugar is responsible, at least in part, to a variety of diseases such as high cholesterol, clogged arteries, diabetes, metabolic syndrome, heart disease, obesity, and breast and colon cancer.

As though that is not enough, we now know that tumors feed off of glucose, so sugar is candy for cancer. Our bodies don't even need added sugars, so long as we have a little fruit.

The first sugar to get rid of is the sugar you drink. I have seen studies indicating that our bodies don't register the calories from our beverages as much as those from food. So if you are trying to lose weight, whether a small or a large amount, this may suffice if you are used to drinking sugary drinks. Drink water, herbal teas, tea, even coffee, but cut out all the drinkable sugar from sodas, fruit juices, and also most flavored coffee drinks.

What changes do you feel compelled to make concerning the food you chose to consume? I now encourage you to look at how you consume food and at what choices you currently make.

Please put the book down and take ten minutes to think about the following three questions.

1. Do I know what is in the food that I eat?

2. Am I eating a diet that supports my health?

3. Can I think of three actions I can take in the next week to improve the health of my diet?

2: Exercise

This section on exercise is based on my 27 years of experience of working out three times a week, most weeks of the year, coupled with my natural curiosity, which led me to research the benefits while I was experiencing them.

I strongly recommend that you find a way to get personalized advice from a professional, but at the very least, get a medical check-up and make sure you do not have any contraindications to exercising.

Personally, I had the benefit of working with a coach at the gym I attended. Since I am working on strength training, a typical session at the gym consists of ten to twelve minutes of an aerobic warm-up, usually running on a treadmill with two to four short sprints, followed by roughly ten exercises targeting specific muscles or muscle groups. I end my program with a bench-pressing program. My personal bench-pressing record is 65kg (143 lbs).

Exercising is the cornerstone of the balance in my life. Through my experiences, I learned early on that the rest of my life will go better if I exercise than if I don't, and that has been enough, most days, to motivate me to exercise. I understand that not everyone is able to self-motivate effectively so let me try to give you some information that might help you do that.

1. Recent studies suggest that inactivity is worse for your health than many illnesses combined so the health recommendations for exercise include moving more throughout the day. Apparently, regular exercise is not enough to offset the effect of an otherwise sedentary life.

   Habits come into play a lot here; it will be a lot easier for you to get a healthy amount of regular exercise if you manage to make it a habit. I will talk more about habits in Chapter 18.

   It will also help you to exercise more if you pick something you like and note how you feel before and after. You will have a much easier time motivating yourself to exercise if you feel better after exercising, and if you are aware of it.

The relationship with willpower goes both ways. It may take willpower to exercise regularly but regular exercise increases your willpower. So think of exercise as having a double benefit. In addition to being a good health investment, it is also your ally to have more willpower to accomplish your other goals.

2. The benefits of exercise are abundantly documented. There are two main categories of exercise:

    -   aerobic exercise, like walking and running, causes your heart rate to increase for a period of time,

        and

    -   strength training, focuses more on strengthening specific muscles.

    Both categories of exercise have different benefits.

    Aerobic exercise is good for improving heart health, increasing metabolism, and helping with mild depres-sion as it has you release feel-good hormones.

    Strength training has various benefits: it reduces the risk of osteoporosis and promotes autonomy, both later in life but also in the prime years, your

30s, 40s and 50s. Having toned muscles helps in lots of areas of life, as menial as bringing in the groceries and as involved as helping a friend move.

Finally, exercising regularly helps with weight manage-ment, which is a huge issue in this day and age. In the US, according to the CDC, almost 40% of adults age 20 and over are obese obese – 71.6% are overweight, including obesity – and obesity also affects one in five children. The numbers in Europe are a bit less dramatic at 10 to 30% of obese adults. Sadly, these numbers are on the rise everywhere.

To end this section on exercise, please take a few moments to ask yourself the following diagnostic questions:

1. Am I exercising at all at the moment?

2. If yes

   a. Am I exercising with enough regularity?

   b. Am I getting a good mix of aerobic exercise and strength training?

3. If no

   a. Can I identify how come I don't?

   b. Can I think of ways to do at least a little bit of exercise?

3: Sleep

More and more people report sleep issues. If you are one of the lucky few who are happy with their sleep quantity and quality, you can skip to the next section.

If you are still reading, I will assume that your sleep situation is not ideal. Sleep is a multi-faceted issue; thus, this book is not the place for a comprehensive study of sleep. I nonetheless invite you in this section to look your relationship to sleep right in the eye.

If like many people you are just hanging out on life's crazy treadmill, many types of sleep issues might bother you. You might have trouble falling asleep; you might have trouble staying asleep; you might wake up not feeling rested even though the night seemed to have been long enough; and then there is the whole issue of how much is enough. Very few of us actually ask that question and many people believe some version of the statement "sleep is a waste of time."

This is simply not true! Many studies illustrate this.

Lack of sleep lowers your sex drive, ages your skin, makes you more forgetful, impairs your judgment, and is detrimental to your health. Lack of sleep can also be dangerous. Several studies show that driving while sleep-deprived is just as dangerous as drunk driving.

Some studies show that sleep deprivation is as bad as smoking, and others indicate that it increases smoking.

If you consistently feel that your sleep is not restful, I recommend that you investigate whether you might have sleep apnea, a common disorder in which you have one or more pauses in breathing or shallow breaths while you sleep. This can perturb your sleep and can cause you to feel drowsy during the day. People with sleep apnea are at higher risk for car crashes, work-related accidents, and other medical problems. If you have it, it is important to get treatment.

Are you getting the point that both quality and quantity of sleep is important?

In this section, I want you to focus on understanding YOUR sleep needs and the conditions that encourage quality rest. In Part III you will decide what actions to take. If you have bigger sleep issues, I urge you to look for more specialized advice.

The first thing to realize is that sleep needs vary greatly among people. Some lucky few can function perfectly well on a few hours of sleep per night, while others need eight, nine, or even ten hours of sleep every night to feel fully rested and able to function to their full potential.

So you first must ask, "How much sleep is enough for me?" Getting enough sleep on a consistent basis is my personal Achilles' heel with my higher than average sleep needs; I am happiest and most productive when I sleep eight to nine hours. I used to often get only six to seven for a few days at a time and then catch up on weekends and sleep experts frown at this. So even if I have made *some* progress on this issue recently, I'm right here with you!

Sleep is a crucial part of self-care. To determine if you are getting enough sleep, note whether you can wake up without an alarm clock and answer the following questions:

- How many days a week do I wake up before my alarm goes off?

- How many days a week do I feel rested enough to go about my habitual activities comfortably?

- How many times per week do I reach for a stimulant, coffee for example, as a pick-me-up?

- How many times per week do I find myself snapping at someone or over-reacting in some way? Could it be that lack of sleep is the culprit?

From your answers to the questions above, what is your impression now of how you are doing with sleep? Are you satisfied with how well and how much you sleep or are you feeling like you could benefit from improving your sleep conditions?

To improve your sleep, there are things you can do, and the sleep doctors have a host of recommendations.

An obvious one is exercise. People who exercise regularly report fewer sleep issues. Some of it is that simple!

Another one is meditation. I will talk about meditation more in the next section. For now, just note that it has a positive impact on sleep quality and quantity.

If your problem is that you have trouble falling asleep because of thoughts running through your head about what you need to do in the future, an immediate tip is to take a pen and paper and write it down. That allows you to let it go, knowing that you can access it in the morning.

Creating and maintaining routines will help you get more rest. A morning routine can help start your day on the right footing no matter how good or bad your night was, and an evening routine can help set the stage for a restful night. If you have children, you have surely heard the advice that babies need a calming routine to sleep well. Why would it be different for adults?

You also need to consider your sleeping environment. In a nutshell, experts recommend that your bedroom be reserved for sleep and sex. This means there shouldn't be a computer, TV, or other electronics in your bedroom. This is for two reasons: it removes work and obligations from your sleep environment, and also the light, sound and pulsation of electronic devices could be detrimental to the quality of your sleep.

Obviously, in order to get quality sleep, your bed better be comfortable. On a scale from one to ten, how comfortable would you say your current bedding is? If your answer is below a seven, I encourage you to invest in a more comfortable bed.

The sleep doctors also have several rhythm-related recommendations. They recommend that you maintain a regular sleep-wake schedule; expose yourself to light during the day and limit light exposure in the evening; don't eat, drink, or nap too much too close to bedtime; and limit caffeine, alcohol, nicotine, and other chemicals that interfere with sleep.

I really urge you to prioritize your sleep.

4: Cultivating Good Health

If you consider your eating habits carefully, have taken time to do some research and picked a healthy eating plan that works for you; if you exercise regularly, including both aerobic exercise and some kind of strength training; if you manage your sleep habits so that you have enough quality sleep, then you are already well on your way to cultivating good physical health.

In this section, I encourage you to think about prevention as well. I continue to share some of the strategies that have worked for me and encourage you to find solutions that work for *YOU*!

To take supplements or not to take supplements?

There is a huge market for supplements: to sleep better, to be more awake, to have better digestion, and to prevent this or that. There are endless possibilities.

Attitude towards supplements are quite culturally sensitive. They are very different in different places. Some sources equate supplements with expensive urine; some claim that it is impossible to get sufficient nutrition from food nowadays; others claim that if you have a sufficient diversity of high quality foods, you may not need supplements. Part of the answer is individual. What works for you?

I have personally found that taking a few supplements helps me:

- B vitamins: I take B vitamins such as found in Brewer's yeast for example. This has helped me with some mild memory lapses I was having.

- Vitamin D: I live in Northern Europe where the whole population apparently suffers from a lack of Vitamin D because the sun is always lower here than closer to the equator. In addition, there is a lot of literature on how Vitamin D strengthens bones and immunity. So I take Vitamin D.

- Vitamin C: I also take Vitamin C regularly for its antioxidant and immunity-boosting properties.

For all my vitamins, I look for natural forms rather than synthetic forms.

Body Weight

Even though I have touched on weight loss in the food and exercise sections, I wish to emphasize weight management as a preventative measure in its own right.

Indeed, obesity is a growing epidemic with serious health implications. It increases the risk of type 2 diabetes, of cardiovascular problems, even of cancer, not to mention the discomfort and the strain it puts on joints and other body parts.

For a lot of overweight people, switching to healthy eating habits, having a regular habit of exercising in a way that is appropriate for their condition, and getting enough sleep can solve weight issues; others may require medical attention.

Adequate weight management has many advantages: fewer health problems, more stamina, more self-confidence, etc.

Alternative medicine

Allopathic medicine is not geared towards prevention; it works something like this: a patient with a health problem goes to a doctor, who gives the patient treatment for her health issue, and then sends the patient home.

Even though allopathic medicine has brought many benefits to our societies, I have personally been on a quest for a form of medicine that offers preventative solutions to maintain good health.

Allopathic medicine is still there, but I resort to it much less frequently. For example, I used to take progesterone for my pre-menopausal symptoms, but that was causing me digestive issues. So my doctor gave me a treatment for the symptoms. The treatment didn't help. I needed to find a better way!

On my path, I found a doctor who is also trained in homeopathy, and so I took a homeopathic treatment instead of the progesterone, which actually regulated my hormonal cycle better than the progesterone did. I also didn't have those pesky digestive disturbances I started having about six months after starting the progesterone. That worked much better for me. As I started getting into menopause, I started taking an evening primrose – borage supplement, recommended by my naturopath, which seemed to work for me as I had almost no symptoms.

In recent years, I have also used homeopathy to strengthen my immunity. A few winters ago, I had a nasty cold that turned into a sinus infection, like many times before. This time, in a flash of determination, I decided that I wanted to treat it naturally. I had started seeing my homeopathic doctor shortly before this, and she helped me. I took Echinacea, Grapefruit seed extract, vitamin C, and some other homeopathic remedies. My body fought hard, and I eventually beat my sinus infection, but it took a good two weeks and left me pretty exhausted. I didn't know it yet but I would later be rewarded for letting my body heal itself.

Homeopathy is not the only alternative medicine there is. I hear more and more talk about using essential oils, acupuncture, or other natural health practices with good results and without all the side effects of some traditional medications. Some people even advocate doing nothing and letting minor ailments just run their course.

How do *YOU* approach this?

The quality of your living environment

Our living environments are increasingly cluttered with stuff but also with more and more electronics. If you want to streamline your home, Mary Kondo has a wealth of writings on *The life-changing magic of tidying up*. It is harder, however, to clean-up the impact of all the electronics we use.

Whether it is your television or your radio, your cellphone or your Wi-Fi router, the increasingly large menagerie of our electronic gadgets are more pervasive than ever. It is not entirely clear if and how these may harm us, but I think this is one of the areas of research to watch closely.

Somewhat worryingly, there is also a growing buzz about what we breathe and take in through our skin, especially from our cleaning products and cosmetics. On the positive side, there are also more and more recommendations for natural alternatives both for cleaning products and cosmetics.

Given all this, I recommend that you make sure you get enough fresh air and hang out regularly in less connected natural environments, especially if you live in a big urban area. Take a moment now to think about all the easy steps you could take to make your living environment healthier.

Prioritizing your health.

I urge you to think of your health as being the biggest investment you can make!

Living your life in good health versus in bad health is simply incomparable. For example, good health brings you more energy, a more positive outlook and a better mood, giving you more time to do what you want to do instead of going to the doctor or the hospital or being bedridden.

I have done my personal research, and I encourage you to do your own if that will reassure you. There is plenty of information out there, figuring out what to believe is not necessarily an easy job, but I encourage you to trust your intuition.

How I prioritize my own health.

I would like to conclude this section on *YOUR* physical health by telling you a short story about *MY* health. I have always enjoyed reasonably good health; I consider myself lucky in this way.

Nonetheless, I had a lot of "minor" things. The most common thing I had growing up—as I have told you before—was sinus infections, which my allopathic doctor treated with antibiotics. That is what they do for those infections.

As I told you in the section on alternative medicine, I had a sinus infection a few winters ago, which I decided to treat naturally. I succeeded but it wasn't easy.

That same winter I had the flu, with six days of fever, a stomach flu, and probably a couple other things. I treated them all with the same basic premise: I am in good health and my body is resourceful!

Each time, my resolve to mobilize my body's resources grew stronger. When I had the flu, I just went on sick leave and stayed in bed for the time of my fever. I did not take any medicine, nothing for the fever or the symptoms, just focused on resting and hydrating.

The first morning I woke up fever-free, I felt like I was coming out of hibernation or something. I thought to myself, "I forgot to enjoy all the days I was fever-free!" When I had the stomach flu, I did the same—rested and tried to stay hydrated, and I took probiotics once I was able to digest again.

I let my body fight one illness after the other, strengthening it with a few supplements. I struggled but felt capable and proud. You might be thinking, "Why would she want to fight so hard when there are pills you can take that make it so easy?"

My answer is this: It has now been several years, and I have had nothing more than a few days of the sniffles a couple of times. I also feel stronger and healthier than ever at over 50 years of age. My body seems to have re-learned to heal itself.

In case you are thinking that I am one of those nuts who reject allopathic medicine, I'd like to say that when I was diagnosed with Deep Vein Thrombosis in 2016, I took the anti-coagulants. I didn't like it, but I did it. After I finished the allopathic treatment, however, I focused on healing and recovering naturally also.

In terms of resources, I like to follow Dr Andrew Weil and also the Sharecare platform. Both will send you frequent emails, if you let them, with all the new information on health promoting behaviors in bite-size pieces.

If you have always been in good health, you may take it for granted and forget to value and nurture it. If you have been struggling with health issues, you undoubt-edly understand the value of good health. In both cases, I recommend that you make it a priority to enhance your health and treat it like your most precious asset!

I mentioned that I get a minor cold, here and there. I find it fascinating that they seem to always come the day after I got really upset about something. Do you think our emotions and our physical health can interfere with one another? I am convinced of that.

In the next chapter, I will discuss your emotional health and show how it can link to your physical health.

Chapter 7

YOUR EMOTIONAL HEALTH

"Those who don't know how
to weep with their whole heart
don't know how to laugh either."
– Golda Meir

"In the last decade or so, science
has discovered a tremendous amount
about the role emotions play in our lives.
Researchers have found that even more than
IQ, your emotional awareness and abilities
to handle feelings will determine your
success and happiness in all walks of
life, including family relationships."
– John Gottman, Ph.D.

> "Happiness is when what you think, what you say, and what you do are in harmony."
> – Mahatma Gandhi

Emotions and Feelings

Feeling them!

Emotions: if there were ever a field that deserves attention, this is it! In many places, emotions are considered incompatible with the workplace or even with family life. Stereotypes are carried around such as "boys don't cry" or "crying is a sign of weakness."

Often, when I see someone crying, someone else is trying to stop them from crying. It is as though the world is afraid of emotions. So people pay professionals, such as myself, to go and cry in the secrecy of a therapy session.

But the truth is your emotions are a language from you to yourself, and you are better off listening to them. How to listen is another matter entirely, and I will get to that a bit later.

First, I would like to clarify a popular misconception. You may have heard of positive emotions—such as joy, cheerfulness, and contentment—and negative emotions such as sadness, anger, or fear. Using the words positive and negative sets the stage for a profound misunderstanding.

It is easy to slip from that to positive emotions are "good" and negative emotions are "bad." Is that what you think? If you answered yes, I will attempt to convince you otherwise.

Emotions are a part of life; they show you that you are affected by the events of your life. They are a very important part of the internal information system that you have. To disown some of your emotions is like disowning a part of yourself, which is yearning to express itself. It is the disowning that is harmful.

I suggest a completely different read on this. Positive emotions may be more pleasant to feel than negative emotions are, but they come out of the same proverbial faucet! If you block off so-called negative emotions, you are left with great difficulty to feel any emotion at all. This prevents you from blossoming and is a very unhealthy way to live.

- Request #4: Do the exercises as they come up. Don't postpone!

Exercise: Please take 20 to 30 minutes to do the following exercise. Think of a different situation for each of the following emotions. Let a situation come to your mind that leads you to feel the emotion, stay with that image for a couple of minutes, and notice how this emotion is manifesting in your body. You may wish to take a few notes in your activity booklet for each emotion.

1. Joy

2. Anger

3. Sadness

4. Fear

5. Cheerfulness

6. Contentment

* * *

I imagine you have experienced the relative pleasantness and unpleasantness of these different emotions, and that is how I invite you to catalogue them. For now, please consider that positive emotions are simply emotions that are pleasant to experience and negative emotions are less pleasant or perhaps downright unpleasant. That's all.

The link between our emotions and our immune system

The psychologist Robert Adler was the first to discover that the human immune system was sensitive to emotions. Thanks to his work, we now know that physical health and emotions are connected. As I have mentioned above, I have observed this link in my life. Have you?

One of the most striking links is that poorly managed stress, as well as other "negative" emotions, weakens our immune response. This is true for a variety of ailments from the common cold all the way to heart attacks. For reoccurring "negative" emotions, the risk for cardiovascular diseases is analogous to the risk from smoking or high cholesterol.

Anxiety, in particular, has been scientifically linked with illness and recovery. The issue is not so much the emotions you feel, but how you deal with them, and there are things you can do to manage your stress and anxiety. Mindfulness has become extremely popular for that.

Mindfulness for dummies: here, now, and without judgment.

"Yesterday is history; tomorrow is a
mystery. Today is a gift, which is
why we call it the present."
– Bill Keane

The best strategy I can recommend for when you are feeling an emotion, any emotion but especially unpleasant emotions, is to be with it in the moment, to become familiar with how it feels in your body, to observe it; in other words, to cultivate mindfulness.

If you have practiced mindfulness before, this part will likely be familiar to you, but if you're anything like me, every reminder to be mindful and kind towards yourself is always welcome.

Mindfulness can be cultivated by having a regular practice: setting a time, daily, to sit and observe your breath, and bring back your attention to your breath when your mind wanders. As you are probably aware, mindfulness has become quite a buzzword, and so often buzzwords get a bit robbed of their intimate meaning. For the moment, let's look at the various attitudes one can consciously wear to approach one's difficult internal states.

The first quality you can cultivate is kindness towards yourself, unconditional friendliness. This does not necessarily come easily even though it is simple enough to spell out, but it is really the most effective response to your unpleasant internal states.

When you are feeling difficult emotions, two things often happen simultaneously: your brain starts looking for elements confirming the validity of this state, and you resist feeling what you are feeling.

The most effective attitude that you can bring to those times is a kind and mindful presence to what is already there. The practice of being present to all internal states as they occur hinges on the ability to be present to what is already there rather than escaping towards what you wish for.

The BBC Family and Education News did a short piece on mindfulness in schools and a video about it went around Facebook for a while. The video showed six- and seven-year-olds stating what mindfulness means:

- "The whole point of mindfulness is where you calm down and relax."

- "Mindfulness is where we have to calm down after playtime and get back into learning, by using our senses and working together."

- "It makes me breathe out all of the things I had to worry about."

- "You really think about your thoughts."

- "Otherwise I would be excited and wouldn't be able to do my work."

Jon Kabat-Zinn, the founder of the Mindfulness-Based Stress Reduction movement (MBSR), lists the qualities of being that make up a mindful presence. He calls the following qualities "the soil in which you will be cultivating your ability to calm the mind and see more clearly."

Non-Judging is about connecting to the impartial, honest but kind, witness that is within all of us. People often generate judgments about their experiences and feelings, almost as a habit. See if you can try observing with impartiality the fact that you are judging, if and when that happens. When you find yourself judging, try not to judge the judging.

Patience is an understanding that things unfold in their time and, as such, is a form of wisdom. See if you can be intimate with impatience when it arises, as you must begin with what is already present, as opposed to what you wish were present. Simply notice when you are feeling impatient, whether with yourself or with another. See if you can bring a spirit of curiosity to it, rather than judgment.

To bring a **Beginner's Mind** to a situation is to remember that you have never been here and now before. Each moment is unique. Just because you have had a similar experience before doesn't mean the experience will repeat itself. See if you can bring freshness to the many encounters in your life, perhaps even with close friends or family members.

Trust goes with self-reliance. When you pay attention to your own body and become intimate with your mind and how it works, you can then begin to trust your own sense of what is best for you. The best response you can give to the situation will emerge from the intimate encounter with your internal states.

Acknowledging and Letting Be go together as they are closely related. This attitude allows you to see things as they are, not as you would like them to be. This does not mean that you will not take action later, to change what doesn't work for you; but the first step is to acknowledge what is, to acknowledge your internal state and let it be, long enough that you can see clearly what it is telling you. Non-judgment is critical here as it prevents getting caught up in blame, either toward yourself or toward others. It is important to see clearly what is happening before deciding what action to take, if any.

The key concept here is "cultivate." These attitudes are not acquired once and for all; you need to cultivate them over and over, especially when you notice that a given attitude is *not* present. You may notice that you are *im*-patient, or that you are focused on what you *want* to be true, rather than what is. In order to cultivate an attitude, you may have to become intimate with its opposite.

A simple way to cultivate mindfulness is to remember to take small breaks throughout your day, and follow your breath for a few moments. Notice what happens without looking for anything in particular. When you become aware that you're on automatic pilot, without judging yourself for it, take a breath and wake up if only for a moment.

Difficult Emotions

So you have emotions and feelings, and some of them are more comfortable than others! I truly want to emphasize that difficult emotions have their place in an otherwise happy and fulfilled life.

As you saw in the section on mindfulness, there is a set of attitudes that you can cultivate to help you go through the rough patches in life; there is no magic trick to get rid of your unpleasant emotions, nor is it desirable to have that.

When you really feel a feeling, you can open up the faucet of all your feelings; while conversely, when you resist a feeling, you clog up the faucet. Since all your emotions give you some information, it definitely behooves you to become intimate with that information, before you can respond to the emotion.

If these difficult emotions are too much for you, it is possible that you could benefit from therapeutic support. You might not be familiar with what therapy is or you might think it is only for people who are crazy in some way so let me paint a different picture. As a therapist, I will work with anyone who is struggling with issues in their life that impact their ability to enjoy their present life to the fullest. These issues often find their roots in the past and together with my clients, after exploring how these issues are actually occurring in their life, we look at how to experiment with new ways of being that lessen the impact of that past.

I offer therapy sessions over zoom and you can find out more about all that right here:

https://eudokima.com/therapy

Breathing

Sometimes you don't want to become intimate with that difficult state. Sometimes you don't have the time, such as a few seconds before going on stage, at the start of an exam, or in a performance evaluation. Sometimes, you need a quick fix to appease yourself.

Breathing is directly linked to your emotions. When you are stressed out, your breathing accelerates. When you relax, it slows down to its natural rhythm. So your emotional life influences your breathing, and your breathing can influence your emotions. By focusing on your breathing, you can replace an anti-stress pill. You may wonder how to do that.

Meet your diaphragm!

Do you know where your diaphragm is? To locate it, find the lowest part of your sternum and place your thumb right below that. Did you find it? Keep your thumb there.

Now I invite you to take three deep breaths while keeping your thumb on your diaphragm. As you inhale, see if you can push against your thumb, and as you exhale, feel your thumb go back down. Take three deep breaths in this way. If you have really found your diaphragm, you will almost certainly find that even three breaths have had an impact and that you feel more serene.

There is a brilliant Ted Talk related to this called *The surprising secret to speaking with confidence* by Caroline Goyder. I encourage you to watch it.

The power of deep-breathing is really quite something, but as you may have experienced before, it is precisely when you need it most that you struggle to breathe deeply. When you are stressed out in one way or another, it is physiologically more difficult to breathe deeply as your heart rate is accelerated and your breathing is shallower.

Yet, it is most beneficial precisely when it is most difficult. With a bit of knowledge, discipline becomes slightly more accessible: you can probably will yourself to take three deep breaths with your thumb on your diaphragm whenever your internal states bother you. Try it, and you may become convinced.

Learn to love your emotions

I hope that by now you are open to the idea that your unpleasant emotions are not the enemy to get rid of, but rather a manifestation of something worthy of your attention.

When you can welcome all of your internal states, most of the time, you become more intimate with your internal language and can then make choices that align with your core self. For some, this comes naturally and for others it comes after a lot of dedicated attention.

But, do not fear the journey of learning what works for you. This journey stretches you and allows you to wake up to more: when you are able to really feel an emotion and go through it in awareness, you end up transformed on the other side. I have been on this journey for over three decades, and the benefits are far greater than what I can convey with words.

Part of the journey is learning to acknowledge difficult emotions and let them live enough to become intimate with them. Another part of the journey is learning to cultivate more positive emotions so as to have a more satisfying balance of positive and negative emotions, of pleasant and unpleasant emotional states.

The Science of Happiness

"When I was 5 years old, my mom always told me that happiness was the key to life. When I went to school, they asked me what I wanted to be when I grew up. I wrote down 'happy.' They told me I didn't understand the assignment and I told them they didn't understand life."
– John Lennon

Since the mid 1990's, the field of positive psychology has really flourished. Before going into some of the lessons you can learn from that, let me first clarify what positive psychology is not.

For a long time, I thought positive psychology boiled down to a shallow recommendation that if you force yourself to see the glass half full, you will be happier. I knew in my heart of hearts that this was not going to work for me and probably not for a lot of other people either.

The field has now come into the public domain, but I still encounter people who hold a belief resembling the one I refer to above. This is NOT what positive psychology is.

Historically, the field of psychology concerned itself with psychopathology, with negative emotions, their implications and helpful responses. The field of positive psychology, by contrast, uses experimental research methods to determine those behaviors and strategies that increase positive emotions.

There is abundant literature on the topics I cover below, and there are many available sources if you wish to deepen your knowledge of one or more of these topics. In this section, I am helping those who are new to this topic become more familiar with its teaching and reminding and reengaging those of you who are already familiar with it.

The field of positive psychology brings a flurry of scientific studies, giving us many strategies for experiencing more positive emotions and handling our difficult emotions in ways that are both more comfortable and also more effective.

I will describe five such strategies.

Coping

It indeed seems unavoidable that life will keep throwing all sorts of stuff at you—some quite difficult and some even downright painful.

The kind of happiness that I strive for, and that I encourage *YOU* to strive for is one that is compatible with your actual life, not some ideal version of it. So from that perspective, it is useful to learn better ways to cope with difficult events. A few skills can be used for this purpose.

Breath meditation works to appease yourself. Just take one minute to focus on breathing deeply. You can also use the diaphragm breath from the last section. You can do this anytime, anyplace.

How about right now, right where you are? Can you take one minute with your breath?

Another thing you can do that doesn't always come naturally, but can be learned, is to regulate how you feel. This may sound amazing or completely absurd if you have never encountered this idea before.

The first thing to notice is that your thoughts have a big impact on how you feel. You can experience that for yourself right now! In fact you have already done this when you brought up six different emotions earlier in this chapter. But let's confirm this now.

Just bring to mind any one of the difficult events going on in many parts of the world. If you think of terrorist attacks, of waves of a pandemic, of climate disturbances and their implications, think of the broken families, the people who suffer, the children who are orphaned, the state of the world and of mankind; if you think of human responsibility in all these things, how does this make you feel? It tends to make me feel sad and fearful mostly. I've also heard of a lot of people who feel angry about all this. Can you feel it? Do you notice that these thoughts do not trigger happy emotions, but rather the opposite?

Now I would like you to turn your attention to something you look forward to, maybe a vacation, a happy event, family time or alone time depending on what you crave more; think of something you look forward to and imagine it in as much detail as you can. Spend a couple of minutes with those thoughts.

* * *

Can you feel how different it is to think about a painful event and to think about something you look forward to? This indicates that if you could control your thoughts, then you would be in much better shape for getting a handle on your feelings.

You can develop skills that help you regulate your emotions. It is very empowering to feel like your happiness is in your own two hands!

Like I said above, if you have never encountered this idea before, you may be filled with disbelief. I certainly wish I had learned some of this stuff earlier in my life; it would have saved me a lot of misery. But that is the path I have since taken, and it really makes a difference.

> "The mind can make heaven out
> of hell and hell out of heaven."
> – John Milton

Changing your thoughts is not easy because for evolutionary reasons, our brains tend to gravitate towards negative events.

- The bad news is it will take focus, time, and patience.

- The good news, though, is that practice does help.

The four tips below will help you to manage your thoughts in such a way as to manage your emotions:

1. Situation selection

This means avoid situations that evoke negative thoughts and/or feelings. If a horror movie makes it hard for you to sleep and you have important sleep needs, you can just avoid watching horror movies.

This may seem obvious, but many of us keep doing the same things, somehow deluded into thinking that the effects might change. For me, going to bed too late is my biggest tripping point, and yet when I don't get enough sleep, I don't feel good. Can you think of such examples in *your* life?

The next three tips are for when you are already in a situation that is causing you negative emotions.

2. Labeling your emotions

The second tip is very simple. It turns out telling yourself that you are feeling angry or sad or anxious or guilty or jealous or whatever it is at the time lowers its intensity. You just need to label the emotion you are feeling.

For example, if you are stuck in traffic and it's annoying you, try saying to yourself, "Hmmm, this is frustrating."

It won't make it go away, but it just might take the edge off.

3. Attention deployment

This means turning your attention away from the things that trigger negative thoughts, or turning it towards things that trigger positive thoughts.

You just did this! Just because you thought of your next vacation didn't make the terrorists, the pandemic, the floods and droughts or the suffering somehow disappear. But it did make you feel better in that moment.

The last tip is called

4. Cognitive reappraisal

This is a sort of reinterpretation of the situation, and it is also linked with gratitude. Cognitive reappraisal is about looking at all sides of a situation.

For example, if you are feeling tense about a work-related meeting, it might be helpful to think how thankful you are that your job provides you with a roof over your head and food in the fridge. While those items don't directly relate to the meeting, thinking about your job in a positive way, reframing your thinking, helps you view the meeting differently. Also, I think it is very useful to not take some of these things for granted!

Mindfulness meditation

I talked about mindfulness earlier when discussing how to approach feelings and emotions. There are many resources about meditation if you wish to delve deeper but I give you an overview here.

To practice mindfulness meditation, you need to observe what is going on, with intense focus, and in a non-judgmental way. To begin practicing, you can set aside some time to focus on your breath, in a non-judgmental way, and every time you notice that your attention has escaped, which it will, you simply bring it back to your breath, remaining as non-judgmental as possible.

Let me first clear some faulty beliefs that people sometimes have about mindfulness and address some concerns that appear frequently.

You may think:	When in fact:
- It means having no thoughts.	- Mindfulness is about changing your relationship to your thoughts.
- You need to understand it first.	- It is not something you can comprehend with your cognitive mind first; you really have to dive in.
- It will take months or years to see results.	- As little as five minutes a day for five weeks gives measurable results.

You may be concerned with:	A helpful response might be:
- Finding time, space, and availability for regular practice.	- Start with really short periods of practice, one or two minutes a day.
- Setting high expectations.	- Each mindfulness session is new, you have never been here and now before. Hence there is no bad session.

There are many benefits to be reaped from a regular meditation practice, both physical and psychological. It may help to motivate you to start or continue practicing meditation if you know about some of these benefits:

PHYSICAL BENEFITS:	PSYCHOLOGICAL BENEFITS:
- changes the physiological structure of your brain	- lowers stress
- reduces the expression of genes that cause inflammation	- improves sense of well-being
- lowers stress in stressful situations	- increases engagement in the present
- improves heart health (blood pressure, arrhythmia...)	- promotes kindness and compassion
- prevents the shortening of telomeres: it slows down aging and helps prevent the onset of disease – including cancer!	- increases chances of success
- accelerates the cure of psoriasis	- enhances creativity

The practice of mindfulness can increase your chances of success. Why is that? Quite simply, it increases your response flexibility which in turn increases your emotional intelligence.

It gives you just a little more space and time to choose how to react to a situation. This increases how much access you have to your experiences and knowledge, which in turn enhances your creativity, which then increases your chances of success in all areas, including your current quest: to live a better life.

Gratitude

To experience more positive emotions, cultivate gratitude! One of the world's most prominent writers about gratitude, Robert Emmons, defines it as

> "A felt sense of wonder, thankfulness and appreciation for life."

Research shows that people are happier when they cultivate an attitude of gratitude.

Let's see if you can conjure up a feeling of gratitude. First, find something that you like in your life, however small or large will work, but be very specific. For example, I am really happy about my exercise routine.

Next, think about how this has come about. In my example, I attended a gathering three days after moving to a new area, and two women I met told me about a gym and a great personal trainer. I joined that gym and attended it for the next 20+ years.

Finally, think about whom you might have to thank for that, who played a role. In my example, I had moved to that area because of my husband's job, and the gathering had a link to his job, so he played a role. A woman I had met earlier whose husband was a colleague of my husband took me to the gathering, so she played a role. The two women who told me about the gym played a role, and I still work out with one of them. Finally, the hostess of the event played a role. Since I derive enormous benefits from my exercise routine, I feel grateful to all those who contributed to that journey.

The items can be relatively small in importance (e.g., "my co-worker made the coffee today") or relatively large (e.g., "I earned a big promotion"). To make this exercise part of your daily routine, you might find it helpful to write in a gratitude journal before bed.

There is a beautiful Ted talk by David Steindl-Rast, a Benedictine monk who thinks a lot about gratefulness; he calls it gratefulness not gratitude. It is 14 minutes really well spent!

According to him, gratefulness spontaneously appears when two criteria are met: something is freely given to you, and it is valuable to you. The easiest access to gratefulness is then to be grateful for every given moment.

Indeed, every moment is freely given to you, and it is certainly valuable as you cannot receive anything else if you don't have this moment. And this is the road to grateful living. I encourage you to watch the whole talk.

There are many ways to train yourself to live more gratefully. Paying attention to the present moment is one way, reflecting on good things from your day just before bed is another way. There are many, many studies showing that practicing gratitude increases feelings of happiness.

Basically, by giving yourself the space to focus on the positive things in your life, however small, you learn to notice, remember, and savor the better things in life. It may prompt you to pay closer attention to positive events down the road and engage in them more fully— both in the moment and later on, when you can reminisce and share these experiences with others. Reflecting on the cause of the event may help attune you to the deeper sources of goodness in your life.

Many people, when they are not trying to deal with some unpleasant event in the past, are looking forward to a brighter future, thinking *I will be happy when...* I suggest instead that you focus intently on savoring life's little joys. This is truly one of the most important ingredients for happiness.

Savoring happens when you intentionally appreciate the present moment, but it is also possible in the present to savor the memory of positive past experiences or to savor the future by anticipating upcoming positive events.

Savoring the present happens when you live mindfully and relish in the present moment. Whether you are meeting a friend for lunch, listening to music you like, watching a Ted talk you find interesting, reading this book, whatever you enjoy, really enjoy it fully. For sure it takes committed effort to redirect your mind to positive experiences.

It will help to motivate you if you know more about why it matters. So why should you care? Well, there are eight ways that gratitude boosts happiness:

1. Gratitude promotes the savoring of positive life experiences by encouraging you to get more enjoyment and satisfaction out of your circumstances.

2. Expressing gratitude bolsters self-worth and self-esteem.

3. Gratitude helps you cope with stress and trauma: by helping you to reinterpret stressful or negative life experiences and/or by reducing the occurrence of traumatic memories and reducing their intensity. While it may be most difficult to be grateful in times of hardship, it may be most valuable to mobilize gratitude in those circumstances.

4. Expressing gratitude encourages moral behavior, such as being more helpful to others and less materialistic.

5. Gratitude helps build social bonds and strengthen relationships. Grateful, positive people are more likely to be liked by others and to make friends.

6. When you feel grateful, you are less interested in what the Joneses are doing; you engage in less comparison with others.

7. Feeling grateful is not compatible with feeling negative emotions!

8. Gratitude helps counteract the effects of hedonic adaptation. When you remain grateful about positive events in your life, you will maintain the happiness boost these events generate.

A caveat does apply here: it is possible to live too much in the present but I don't think anyone in the western world, except homeless people and Alzheimer patients, is in much danger of that. Nonetheless, it is important to also have goals and pursue them. We will get back to your goals in Part III of this book.

For now, how about you give gratitude a try?

Forgiveness

There is a lot of evidence, both from academic studies and also from the personal development movement in general, on how forgiveness increases happiness.

The thing to understand about holding a grudge towards someone who has hurt you is that the grudge hurts you, not them! The more you hold onto a grudge or a sense of wrongdoing against you, the more you flood your body with chemicals associated with those negative emotions.

Meanwhile, the person you are holding a grudge against is not affected at all. Moreover, should you interact with that person as you are harboring negative emotions, they are more likely to become defensive.

Forgiveness entails letting go of resentment or vengeance toward an offender and making peace with what has happened so that you can move on with your life; it doesn't necessarily mean reconciling with that person.

Research suggests that practicing forgiveness can not only strengthen relationships but also reduce toxic feelings of stress and anger and boost happiness and optimism. In a nutshell, forgiveness reduces feelings of anger and resentment that are not serving a constructive purpose.

This in turn helps to shift your mental attention away from ruminating negative events in your past, which can decrease stress levels. In addition to this, practicing forgiveness encourages you to focus on and appreciate the positives in your life, opening your heart to kindness, beauty, and love, which in turn leads to healthy relationships as well as physical health.

The process of forgiveness takes time and should only be initiated when you feel ready and have had time to grieve the wrong that was done to you.

As I mentioned before, I had a very difficult relationship with my mom, growing up. I felt like she didn't really love me for who I was and didn't even really see me as the person I was. This had all sorts of impacts on my life and I carried around a lot of anger about all that. After many years of therapy, I finally made peace with things and really let go of my resentment, I found forgiveness. In my TedX talk "Finding Happiness: How Forgiving my Mother Radically Changed My Life", I share the near miracles that forgiveness allowed in my life. You can watch my TedX talk here:

https://eudokima.com/tedx

To conclude this section on forgiveness, I'd like to quote Nelson Mandela who, when asked by Bill Clinton how he was able to forgive his jailers, answered, "When I walked out of the gate, I knew that if I continued to hate these people, I was still in prison."

I won't deny that practicing this stuff is hard. Our brains are wired to see problems and to hold onto negative things more than positive experiences. So it can be an uphill battle, but the view from the top is amazing; you can take my word for that!

The last topic for this chapter is self-compassion. You might be interested to know that it is much more effective at getting you to pursue your goals than being hard on yourself. Let's go into that a bit more.

Self-Compassion

"With self-compassion, we give ourselves the same kindness and care we'd give to a good friend."
– Dr. Kristin Neff

Dr. Kristen Neff is an associate professor of human development at the University of Texas and the world expert in self-compassion.

Self-compassion, as defined by Dr. Neff, is made of three separate components:

1. Mindfulness, meaning that we are aware of our experience, rather than ignoring or exaggerating our difficulties.

2. Recognizing our common humanity, which means that even in our suffering, we feel connected with others, rather than feeling isolated and alienated by the suffering.

3. Self-kindness, which means to treat ourselves gently and with understanding, rather than with harsh criticism and judgment.

Most of us are more familiar with self-esteem as a way to motivate ourselves. The unfortunate thing about self-esteem is that it hinges on some notion of performance; self-esteem goes hand in hand with self-criticism.

Maybe you have had the experience of thinking, "I am such a loser!" when you have failed at something of importance to you. It is a carrot and stick approach that leads to a fear-based type of motivation: *I will not be OK if I fail, so I must try harder and succeed in order to be OK.*

If you are familiar with this experience, you may recognize some of the likely effects.

1. You may get somewhat depressed. This does not work wonders for motivation, to say the least.

2. You may lose faith in yourself. As you keep criticizing yourself, you lose your feeling of competence. This is unfortunate as research shows that perceived competence is key for motivation.

3. You may become so afraid of failure that you stop trying. The consequences of failure would be so devastating that it is not worth the attempt.

4. It gives you an illusion of control. When you say to yourself, "I shouldn't have failed!" it seems to imply the possibility of not failing. *If I only did things right, I wouldn't fail.*

Self-compassion is different from self-esteem in that it doesn't hinge on us being better than anyone else or meeting some extraordinary goal. Self-compassion, on the contrary, picks up precisely where self-esteem may let us down, when we fail or feel inadequate.

The real benefit of self-compassion comes when things go wrong. Without self-compassion, when something goes wrong, you might think to yourself, "I'm such a loser." With self-compassion, however, you instead think, "Everybody goofs up now and then," and "In the long run, this doesn't really matter."

Hence self-compassionate people are better able to accept who they are regardless of the degree of praise they receive from others. Self-esteem, on the other hand, only thrives with positive reinforcements.

Yet, a lot of people are afraid of compassion. One reason for this is that they strongly believe that they need their self-criticism to motivate themselves and keep themselves in line; and the Western culture supports that.

Ask yourself right now: how is self-criticism working for you?

When you motivate with self-compassion, the motivation becomes all about wanting health and well-being for yourself and encouraging and supporting yourself toward those goals, whereas self-esteem attempts to motivate with *I am not worthwhile if I fail.*

Moreover, research shows that self-compassion is a very effective motivator. This hinges on these three factors:

1. Self-compassion focuses on self-acceptance, not self-improvement.

   With self-compassion, you fully accept yourself as you are, flaws and all, even though you're not perfect, even though you might fail. Self-compassion is not about self-improvement or evaluating yourself; it is just about accepting who you are, as you are.

2. The paradoxical theory of change.

> "The curious paradox is that when I accept myself as I am, then I can change."
> – Carl Rogers

You may wonder if self-acceptance might mean being passive or complacent? You may think accepting things how they are would not help to motivate you to make a change?

Well, as it happens, when you accept yourself fully, and you embrace who you are, it allows you to see yourself clearly because it is safe to do so. Then, because you care about yourself and don't want to suffer, you're going to try to make changes that make you healthier and happier. With self-compassion, you also know that if you don't succeed, it's still okay.

Self-compassion provides the emotionally sup-portive environment needed for change and growth.

Self-compassion helps with motivation because you tell yourself that you would really like to be happier, more fulfilled, and that you will care for and nurture yourself, regardless of what happens. Yet, you understand that you don't have total control over what happens, and you will just do what you can.

Dr. Neff has a wealth of evidence to show the unambiguous benefits of self-compassion over self-criticism, in diverse areas ranging from parenting to weight loss and goal setting.

Can you treat yourself like you would a dear friend?

* * *

Now that you have learned some strategies for cultivating positive feelings and have worked on your relationship with yourself, you can begin to work on your relationships with others, the topic of the next chapter.

Chapter 8

RELATIONSHIPS

> "Let us be grateful to people who make us happy, they are the charming gardeners who make our souls blossom."
> – Marcel Proust

We all know intuitively that as humans we are a social species: loneliness hurts and human contact feels good. In this chapter, I urge you to take a look at this more closely. What does it mean exactly that we are social?

Evolutionarily Social

Harry Harlow, a psychology professor at the University of Wisconsin at Madison in the 1930s, conducted research on monkeys. The parts of his work best known to the general public are his seminal studies on the mother-infant bond in his monkey population.

These studies brought a completely unexpected discovery at the time. The experimenters put baby monkeys in cages with two devices to act as "mothers." One was made of wire and was rigged up to give milk on demand while the other one was made of cloth and the baby monkey could cling onto it for comfort.

How much time do you think the baby monkeys spent nursing in a 24-hour period?

It turns out they spent only one hour out of 24 nursing; the rest of the time was spent cuddling with the cloth mother.

Harry Harlow and his team were shocked! They said:

"We were totally unprepared to find that the variable of comfort completely overwhelmed and overshadowed all other variables, including those of nursing."

Humans, like monkeys, have a huge need for love and nurturing, and when it is not given to us or when it is given to us in a way that doesn't suit us, we can be quite psychologically damaged. Let me tell you, I see a lot of this in my therapy practice.

We need social connection; it is part of our common humanity. In one experiment, participants are asked which three wishes they would request from a Genie; in an overwhelming majority of cases, people wished for great relationships.

Other studies, which use brain imagery, show that being socially rejected activates the same brain circuits, just as when we experience physical pain!

The Harvard Medical School is running a study that is the longest longitudinal study of adult development. It has been underway for over 75 years. Let's see what they can teach us about this.

The Study of Adult Development at Harvard Medical School

Successive Harvard research teams have been following the lives of 724 men since the 1930's. Year after year, they asked them questions about their professional life, their personal life, and their health, not knowing what would happen. In November 2015, 60 participants were still alive and still participating in the study. More than 2000 children of the original 724 men are now part of the study.

The group was made up of two cohorts: one cohort of sophomores at Harvard, and a second cohort of disadvantaged, non-delinquent, inner-city youths who grew up in Boston neighborhoods. The research teams gathered information using questionnaires, information from the men's physicians, and in many cases personal interviews. Information was gathered about their mental and physical health, career enjoyment, retire-ment experience, and marital quality. The goal of the study was to identify predictors of healthy aging.

As time went by and medical possibilities increased, brain scans were included. They also filmed them discussing their biggest issues with their wives. They even started to talk to the kids. In the early 2000's, they started talking to the wives, who thought it was about time!

George Vaillant, the principal investigator in the study, described the methodology and results in a series of three books. The study is now under the direction of Dr. Robert J. Waldinger at Massachusetts General Hospital. They have gathered thousands of pages of information about the lives of those men and their families.

In a wonderful Ted talk, Robert Waldinger, the current director of the study, asks:

"So what have we learned?"

He then answers his own question:

"There are three main lessons from this study aiming to answer the question of what makes a successful life," and he goes on to describe them.

1. Social relations are good for us and loneliness kills.

People who feel socially connected, whether to their families, to their friends, or to their communities are happier, healthier, and they live longer.

Loneliness is toxic; and, sadly, a lot of people complain of loneliness.

2. Quality not quantity.

It doesn't matter how many friends we have or if we are in a stable relationship, at least not as much as the quality of the relationships we do have. This then affects our health. Living in conflict is bad for our health.

For the 80-somethings in the study, they looked at what was happening to them 30 years prior. You might be surprised to find out that it is not their cholesterol that gave the best prediction of their health 30 years down the line. Nope! It was their level of satisfaction with their close relationships.

Those who were happiest with their close relationships at age 50 enjoyed the best health at age 80!

3. Good relations don't just protect our bodies, they protect our brains.

The 80-somethings who felt that they could rely on their partner kept their memory for longer. This holds true even in relationships that have some conflict. Arguments are okay. What really protects us is knowing we can rely on someone despite arguments.

Thus, nurturing your relationships—which is neither easy, nor sexy, nor glamorous, and it never ends—pays for your well-being, your physical health, and your mental health.

Vaillant's main conclusion is that "warmth of relation-ships throughout life has the greatest positive impact on life satisfaction." Put differently, Vaillant says the study shows that:

"Happiness is love. Full stop."

Taking stock

Given how important social contact is to humans, it is time now to ask yourself how socially connected you feel. I recommend that you take a few minutes right now, that you set a timer for five minutes, close your eyes, and reflect on your connectedness.

Quantity is not the aim here. The feeling of connectedness hinges much more on the quality of human connection, on the depth of what is shared, on the sense of intimacy that comes from being in a caring, warm relationship.

Let yourself feel, right now, how connected you are. Allow for an intuitive response. How connected and how isolated do you feel?

You may feel some of both. Indeed, it is possible that you have deep satisfying friendships, but that you feel estranged from your partner or your family, and this gives you a sense of isolation. The reverse may be true: you may feel very connected at home, but socially more isolated.

At this time, I invite you to really take stock of how connected you feel.

In the next three sections, I will go over different types of relationships to help you get a very clear picture.

Friends

One area of connectedness is our social life. There are many types of people regarding this area. Some prefer one-on-one interactions and close intimate friendships; others like to hang out in groups, big or small, and have a more festive social life made of parties, group dinners, or group outings. There are different levels of intimacy in different settings.

What are your preferred qualities for your social life?

Large groups are usually less conducive to deep and personal sharing. But depending on your personality and also your personal history, that may be what you prefer.

Reflect on your social life: is it as active as you would like? Do you crave more social activities? Do you get together with a close group of friends as often as you would like? Do you enjoy the large crowd scene now and again, or do you socialize out of a sense of obligation?

If you enjoy having a very active social life, how close are you to where you want to be? Try to answer according to how your social life aligns with who you are at your core and not according to what others deem appropriate.

You may have an active social life, but find that you lack true friends. You may shy away from emotional intimacy or may struggle finding others to connect with.

Be curious, how open do you feel in your friendships? Do they have a more casual feel? Or do you feel intimate with your friends? How comfortable are you sharing personal things with your friends?

Personally, I favor one-on-one or small group settings as I am a glutton for emotional intimacy. From my experience, I suggest to *you* that sharing openly can be one of the biggest sources to feeling connected.

I suggest that you be attentive to how you relate to your friends and acquaintances in the next few days and see if you can think of ways to make those relationships more satisfying.

Family

Another area of connectedness is family. This connection is of a different kind as Harper Lee has Jem say in "To Kill a Mocking Bird":

"You can choose your friends but you sho' can't choose your family, an' they're still kin to you no matter whether you acknowledge 'em or not, and it makes you look right silly when you don't."

Family is different from other types of relationships as they are still kin to you no matter, whether you acknowledge them or not. This implies that family relationships can be passionate in a variety of different ways.

Having a satisfying relationship with family, who will be your kin no matter what, can bring a sense of security and connectedness, of being part of a lineage and inscribed in the circle of life.

Having strained family relations can bring hardship and sometimes even tragic consequences: for example recently in France, a man murdered his wife's brother and his whole family, including two young adult children, over an inheritance turned sour!

Without going quite that far, strained relationships with family take a toll; it takes a lot of emotional energy to refuse a connection that is indestructible, whether it is genetic, historical, or both.

Depending on your age, you might have ageing relatives. Most of us are quite affected when our elders leave us. However, regardless of the relationship you entertain with them, they are part of your history. You get your DNA from them.

A lot of people who lose a relative with whom the relationship was strained feel a greater sense of loss from the incompleteness of the relationship.

If you have elderly relatives with whom you have an incomplete relationship, I strongly suggest that you attempt to cultivate peace, using some of the tips from the emotional health chapter (Chapter 7) and see if you might be able to spend a bit more time with them and find some resolution.

You have a shared history with your family; it is the locus of inter-generational transmission. It is up to you to see if sharing some of your present with them may also be either desirable or possible, and perhaps both.

Love

Love relationships can bring out the best and the worst of people. Indeed, the more intimate we get with someone, the more we access our most intimate relational patterns and our deepest wounds as well.

With mixed success, we tend to choose partners who re-create a familiar emotional atmosphere for us, one that we know from our childhood, one that may not be conscious. Sometimes we fall madly in love with people who end up making us very unhappy. And sometimes, it is the opposite: our lover gives us that which we yearned for.

My early relational patterns left me with a belief that I couldn't be loved. I was largely unaware of this being a belief. That is how I saw the world. As I shared in the section on beliefs, this had the very predictable effect: in retrospect, I realized I kept choosing relationships in which I did not feel loved.

It was not until I went through a large amount of personal growth that I was able to expose this belief and modify it. I now share a love with a man, which is more wonderful than what I had ever imagined possible.

What are the ways in which your love relationship reminds you of earlier experiences? Does your love relationship feel more empowering or more stifling? Whatever your answer, know that it is often possible to improve your relationship.

In her book *Committed*, Elizabeth Gilbert offers a very useful metaphor for this, quoting her gem-buyer husband:

"A parcel is this random collection of gems that the miner… puts together. [...] Supposedly, you get a better deal that way—buying them all in a bunch—but you have to be careful, because [... he's] trying to unload his bad gemstones on you by packaging them together with a few really good ones.

For a better deal yet, you have to ignore the perfect gemstones. Just put them away and have a careful look at the really bad stones. Look at them for a long time, and then ask yourself honestly, *Can I work with these? Can I make something out of this?*"

It is very similar for spouses! If you're married, you find that your spouse has lovely, positive qualities, but your spouse also has aspects you can't stand after a while. The question becomes, can you deal with those aspects you don't like?

Sometimes couples get locked into destructive patterns, when their past relational pattern interact in a disharmonious way. Many couples will then decide to separate, only to find that they get into similar issues with their next partner. If your one-upon-a-time heavenly love has turned into a hellish relationship, I really urge you to get support for your couple to look at the transformation that has taken place and unearth the triggers. If things seem irreconcilable, you will be able to have a more peaceful separation and also reduce the chances of going through this whole ordeal again. And in the best of cases, this will rekindle your love in a more realistic and more sustainable context. I also offer couples therapy and I have seen both of these outcomes with past clients. If you are having trouble in your couple and would like to give it a chance, find out more about how I work here:

https://eudokima.com/therapy

Whether you engage in couples work or not, a good question to ask yourself is "What are you looking for in a love relationship?" What kind of person will best complement you? This question can of course not be approached in the same way if you are single or if you are already in a committed relationship.

In all circumstances, however, it is possible to clarify what you are expecting of a love relationship, even one that is already underway. Clarifying expectations is one way for relationships to grow to the next level.

Breakdowns

Sometimes you may find that it is not possible to bridge differences. A relationship may come to a breaking point. It may be too late for couple's therapy to rekindle the flame.

In that case, it is important to cultivate peace within your own heart. If this is the case for you, I encourage you to seek to forgive both yourself and the other person. Your impossibility to connect often stems from a limitation that you are not aware of. Couple's work can also be useful in this case.

At times when it may seem that you cannot find connection with fellow humans, you might look for other connections. Perhaps you can find inspiration in the next chapter.

Chapter 9

SPIRITUALITY AND MEANING

"Just as a candle cannot burn without fire,
men cannot live without a spiritual life."
– Buddha

"The most beautiful thing we can
experience is the mysterious. It is the
source of all art and science."
– Albert Einstein

"It is not length of life; but depth of life."
– Ralph Waldo Emerson

"The longest journey is the journey inwards."
– Dag Hammarskjöld

"Most of us spend our lives as if
we had another one in the bank."
– Ben Irwin

"A piece of us is in every
person we can ever meet."
– Stephen R. Covey

Spirituality Light

I am including a chapter on spirituality and meaning even though I haven't been spiritual for all that long, and I am still feeling my way. Note that I am not talking about religion; I am not a religious person, yet I do respect everyone's individual beliefs as long as they imply a similar kind of respect.

In my mind, organized religion has little to do with spirituality and a lot more to do with like-minded community. Thus, I am discussing spirituality not religion and as such, I give an overview of my spirituality-light approach and how it contributes meaning to my own life.

If you have been practicing spirituality for a long time, I recommend that you bring a beginner's mind here and see if there is anything new for you in this chapter. If you are a spiritual beginner, welcome to the journey!

In this chapter, I will be sharing my approach, my reflections, and some of my beliefs.

I invite you, as I do everywhere in this book, to be curious about your own beliefs and the extent to which my path resonates for you.

Inspiration

The first aspect of my spiritual life lies in what inspires me. For this purpose, I use the meaning of the verb *inspire* (v.), which in Middle English was also used to mean "breathe or put life or spirit into the human body."

So what would you answer to the "What for" question? What are some of your beliefs about why we are here, what our purpose is?

Do you think that we are part of something bigger? Do you think, like Elon Musk, that we might be part of a big simulation? Or do you prefer to think of us as having free-will or purely being a random event in the world with no particular meaning or purpose?

Personally, I have begun thinking more and more about how we are all connected here on earth, and how important it is to start reflecting that in our ways of living. I don't really know about a bigger purpose and certainly find it hard to envision us being part of a simulation.

One idea particularly helps me to find inspiration daily, and that is to remember that thoughts become things. If you are not yet convinced of this, I strongly encourage you to consider it.

If you have a lot of negative self-talk, chances are that your circumstances match that. It is of course easy to interpret that backwards and to think that the fortunate people have happy thoughts because they are fortunate.

I invite you to pay attention to your thought patterns and to consider modifying those that do not support the life you are aiming to build.

Quite possibly, the universe has your back!

Beauty

Planet Earth offers a lot of natural beauty that might inspire you! In this section, I am inviting you to consider awe, a sense of wonder that emerges when faced with natural beauty.

Depending on where you live, you may have access to various beautiful natural sites, or you may travel to some on your vacations. At the very least, you may have pictures of such places on your computer.

Whether you like forests, the sea or mountains, there is a common aspect to all those sites, which is that they are much larger than our comparatively small person, and if you are attentive, a feeling can emerge of grand appreciation, of recognition that being in the presence of this natural grandeur provides you with a gift: a feeling of awe.

The research on feelings of awe suggests that it has an impact on well-being and may even impact our health.

Aside from the feeling of awe, which I strongly recommend that you open yourself up to, being in nature is associated with many benefits. The benefits can be cognitive, such as helping with short-term memory or with sharper thinking and creativity; they can be health related, such as stress-reduction, increasing well-being, even immune system boosts, and possible anti-cancer effects.

If, like most people, you find yourself without easy or immediate access to beautiful natural sites, you may have easier access to a park, or you may have a small garden with a few plants or trees.

I encourage you, at the very next available opportunity, which may be right now, to go and interact with any amount of nature for five minutes. Just be with nature for five short minutes and just pay attention to how you feel.

***

How was that? Do you feel more connected or more grounded?

One grand natural manifestation that I know you have access to is the sky. Every day the sun rises and sets, and every night, stars and planets are more or less visible, depending on how much light pollution you are exposed to, or cloud cover.

I am often amazed at the way the clouds and the sun interact in the sky and what images that creates. It is a small source of appreciation in my everyday life, and it is free, all it requires is to pay attention.

Why don't you try looking at the sky right now, what do you see? Even on a cloudy day, there can be wonders to be seen, just above your head, which can bring you a sense of connection.

Self-Realization

I believe spiritual alignment parallels self-realization. What do I mean by that? I don't mean that one should be selfish and look to serve one's every need. No.

I mean that looking for your core self to shine is the path to your spiritual alignment.

Perhaps this is clearer put in terms of purpose. What is your purpose, your mission in life? For myself, I have found my mission: to lead people to discover and finally Experience Their TRUE Happiness, by discovering their own keys to a happy life within their environment. And this is why I have written this book.

My deepest wish is that reading this book will inspire you to take concrete steps to improve your life, to live in a way that is more aligned with your core values and with your environment.

You may have a sense of your purpose already, but if you don't, I suggest that you open your activity booklet or take a piece of paper and a pen, set a timer for ten minutes and write: "What I most wish to accomplish in this lifetime is..." and just write whatever comes to you. If you feel stuck and nothing is coming to you, start writing anything—your shopping list, a letter to a friend, anything that can make you start writing.

Just keep in mind that you are trying to get to what you most wish to accomplish in this lifetime. If you need to, take another set of ten minutes and perhaps even another. At some point, you are sure to come to elements of what brings meaning to your life, what gives you a sense of purpose.

This is one way to listen to what I like to call the *whisper within* although you may access it in other ways. In Part III, I will go over a number of actions you can take to get closer to the keys to your fulfillment. Meanwhile, for the purpose of self-realization, I invite you to try on the perspective that the best way to show up in this lifetime is in alignment with your inner truth.

There are so many ways that this inner truth may have become less accessible through your early and not so early life experiences. If you are reading this book, I assume that you can relate, at least to some extent, to struggling to hear the whisper within and having to search for your true self inside.

The path to self-realization is not clearly laid out. It is the result of a process of discovery, of self-discovery. Think of yourself as an explorer: you are living your life, day in and day out, and alongside the daily routines that are already in place, you are keeping your senses awakened to gather more information about where the next step may lie for you in your situation.

It is a very personal path, and I can totally support the idea that sometimes it takes courage to walk that talk. This path is about daring to be yourself! There may be ways in which you are not quite living in agreement with your inner truth, and it may be downright scary to contemplate that.

Sometimes it takes courage to face your fears. You may feel inadequate at first as you start living more in agreement with yourself; you may experience loyalty conflicts between the way you "think you should be" and the way you simply are. This is a path of personal development.

You may be more or less advanced on this path and so this might make more or less sense to you as you read. Worry not, it is a path we can all travel and to which it is useful to bring a beginner's mind. The path of self-realization is a never-ending one; it is a life-journey.

As many journeys, this one is fraught with great rewards and sometimes great distresses. It is useful to remember your commitment in those moments. In Part I, I talked about commitment and all that goes with it. Remember that you can go and review the principles laid out in Part I any time you find yourself struggling with your commitment.

Causes

One of the ways to tap into self-realization is to get involved in a cause you believe in. By engaging in activities linked to that cause, you will very likely derive a sense of purpose.

Do you have a favorite cause that you engage with? Actions you take in the name of something you consider a worthy goal? My favorite cause is engaging in small behaviors that are beneficial to the environment.

I think it is pretty amazing to think about everything that our planet offers and how we are taking too much from it in the developed world. This happens at the expense of the future possibilities for our own children later, but even more alarmingly, at the expense of large, already economically disadvantaged populations. If you wish to see what I mean, I recommend Leonardo Di Caprio's documentary *Before the Flood*

Yet there are more optimistic stories also and one of those is told by the French film: *Tomorrow.*

The movement emerging from the movie suggests five everyday actions for a better tomorrow for all:

1. Eating more organic food and less meat

2. Opting for a renewable electricity supplier

3. Buying from local and independent sources

4. Choosing an environmentally responsible bank

5. Reducing, re-using, recycling, repairing, sharing

In my day-to-day life, I am quite engaged along most of those dimensions. I engage in many small actions to reduce my consumption of fossil fuel energy or the quantity of trash I generate. And every action I take linked with this cause brings me joy.

What cause can you engage with that will bring YOU joy?

The Power of Now

On your spiritual path, one of the most powerful approaches is to cultivate attention to the present moment. Eckhart Tolle, in his wonderful book *The Power of Now: A Guide to Spiritual Enlightenment*, says

"Time isn't precious at all, because it is an illusion. What you perceive as precious is not time but the one point that is out of time, the Now. That is precious indeed. The more you are focused on time—past and future—the more you miss the Now, the most precious thing there is."

Of course, if you want to go forward in your life, plan things, and accomplish goals, you must do more than focus on the present moment. This much is obvious. It seems fair to say that in our western developed world, we err on the side of either being stuck in the past or being too forward-looking. Hence for most of us, learning to be in the present moment is a worthwhile endeavor.

I suggest that you can increase your attention to the present moment, even as you make peace with the past and work towards your future oriented goals.

Being in the present moment implies a form of letting go. My experiences, both personal and with my clients, lead me to believe that this is one of the more difficult things to grasp. Often my clients who are angry about the way things are think that to let go means to stop caring about everything and just go with the flow. That is not quite what I mean.

In all individual moments, there is the way things are, and that is fixed in that instant. What is not fixed is your response to what is: your affect, your intentions. That is where you have power: the power to BE with what is and AIM to move in the direction that is more supportive of your personal path at the same time.

As I write this, I am thinking of a client I work with. She is very irritated with the management of the organization she works for. According to her, they don't do what they should; that is not how one should manage.

She can see that this is detrimental to the organization as a whole, and she suffers greatly from this state of things, as she continually WANTS things to be different than they are. Her challenge is to separate what IS from what actions she can take either for herself or for others in the organization. The inner state of WANTING things to be different from what they already ARE is one of the most frustrating states to be in.

Cultivating presence in the moment is a powerful antidote to this frustration. One way to come back to the present moment is to use Mindfulness and Breathing as described in Chapter 7. Another simple way to connect to the present moment is to connect to greater things. For example, connecting with nature is also a direct way to presence.

When you find yourself struggling with the way things are, and if you don't want to look inside yourself, see if you can go outside, or at the very least look outside, and focus your attention on the greatness of nature or the seeming infinity of the sky. In Part III, you will find several activities that will help you to cultivate presence.

Living Together

I include some approaches to living together as essential to my notion of a healthy spiritual life.

We live in times where togetherness seems problematic at some aggregate levels. Recent political events, at the time of the first edition of this book, such as the Brexit vote and the election of Donald Trump, quite aside from any political debate, seem to indicate an increase in *Us vs Them* attitudes.

There have allegedly never been more walls, barriers, and fences in the world since the Middle Ages. These dividers mark the separation between Us and Them and research shows that these separations lead to a phenomenon called infrahumanization. This term, coined by Jacques-Philippe Leyens, denotes a tacitly held belief that one's in-group is <u>more human</u> than an out-group, which is <u>less human</u>.

Living together may hence not be easy when historical facts make it easy to pit segments of population against one another. So in order to cultivate the ability to live together, you must examine your attitude towards differences.

We are all different, but we all have similarities too. Our biggest similarity is that we are all human. The documentary by that same title exemplifies this fact beautifully!

Yet there is a tendency, in political leaders and people in general, to point out differences. Racial and religious differences can be a huge source of conflict. And moving beyond those differences can open up new possibilities.

A lovely Danish advertisement went viral on Facebook and showed people who were standing inside squares drawn on the floor, according to usual categorizing.

The video shows a group of diverse Danes who discover that, beneath the surface, they have more in common with each other than what their outward appearances might suggest. The video starts with: "It's easy to put people in boxes: there's us and there's them. The high earners and those just getting by. Those we trust and those we try to avoid. There are the new Danes and those who have always been here."

Then they ask participants to step forward under new labels: step-parents, people who have been bullied, people who have bullied, those who have had sex within the past week and the "boxes" begin to disappear and shared experiences give way to new groupings.

The video concludes with a profound realization:

"Maybe there's more that brings us together than we think."

So when you find yourself focusing on differences, I invite you to search for one area of commonality.

Sometimes that can be difficult, but even then, you can still cultivate an attitude of tolerance. If you cannot feel the commonality, maybe you can still grant the other person the right to exist.

Some people may find it easier to be tolerant due to the values they were raised with or their life experience. If you have a history of not tolerating differences, then maybe this is a good growth edge to focus on.

Forgiveness has a place in this too. What may be in the way of tolerance might better be approached by cultivating forgiveness. I talked about forgiveness in Chapter 7: holding on to grudges or wrongdoings doesn't do anyone any good! It makes the person holding onto those things less happy and less able to connect with other fellow humans.

I put the question to you: what form of spirituality can survive an inability to consider living together as a worthy goal?

My personal answer: none!

Money

You may find it surprising to find money in a chapter on spirituality. Please bear with me for a few minutes and see if you might be able to join me on this.

Money is the subject of many a love-hate relationship. Possibly it always has been, but current times make this even more likely. There has never been as much wealth as there is across the planet and inequalities have never been as large.

If you think about it, what is money?

It is only a means of exchange! This means of exchange has only two purposes. One is to allow trading without having to bother with finding someone to trade the right goods with: it standardizes value. The other is to allow saving for delayed spending: it stores values.

Where spirituality and money meet is when you can understand that money is a symbol of human productivity and achievement. When people bring their passion and talent to what they do, and they earn an honest income doing that, then the money they receive in exchange is just that, a symbol of their productivity and achievement.

"Money is like a sixth sense
without which you cannot make
complete use of the other five."
– W. Somerset Maugham

Now is a great time to ask yourself, what is your relationship to money like? Is it peaceful? Are you wanting more or do you feel that you have enough? Do you find money evil or otherwise disgusting or do you appreciate earning it the way you do and are you appreciative of what it allows you to do?

Often we have a view on money that comes from our upbringing and also from what happens in the society we live in. And sometimes what we see makes money look bad.

For example, the scandals in the French presidential election in 2017 is one of many instances involving large sums of money that are suspected to have been somehow embezzled by people who already have way more than enough. This contributes to giving money an image of something evil. The amount of tax avoidance done by rich people also attaches characteristics such as dishonesty and greed to money, as though they would necessarily go together.

What I suggest here, is to remember that money and greed are not the same thing, even if it is pretty ugly when they meet. I recommend that you both un-demonize and de-sacralize money, that you remember what money is: a means to standardize and store value.

In the context of developing spirituality for a more aligned experience of life, I recommend reflecting on how money connects you to your purpose.

For example, my professional activities are all aligned with my mission to lead my clients to discover and finally Experience Their TRUE Happiness, by discovering their keys to a happy life within their environment. In that sense, when I get paid for my work, I feel connected with the greater purpose that I am working towards and that is joyful. Regarding spending the money, a lot of my decisions are rooted in my environmental engagement and that is also joyful.

This too can be a journey but if you can earn your money in ways that are aligned with your purpose or a cause you believe in and that are compatible with your spiritual engagement; if you then spend it to create a life that reflects such a purpose and such an engage- ment, then I believe that you have succeeded to un- demonize and de-sacralize money.

* * *

In Part II, I have covered several areas of focus that will contribute to your sense of well-being and connection. I talked about Physical Health, Emotional Health, Relationships, and Spirituality and Meaning.

In Part III, I will go over a selection of 23 different activities for different areas of your life. It's time to roll up your sleeves and try some actions. Remember that you will not know how something works for you if you don't try it!

While I have given my best effort to guide you to reflect deeply on how you live your life and how you would like to improve it, I have given you some information, some tips, some suggestions, and in Part III I will give you some structured activities.

Perhaps you are finding that this is a lot for you to do alone and you would like more support to travel this journey. That is exactly why I have created The "Experience Your TRUE Happiness" Haven. This is a safe and warm space in which I will guide you through a similar yet enriched journey, it is a group program to add an extra layer of support and companionship. If you would like to find out more about this program, it is right here:

https://eudokima.com/the-haven

Part III

GETTING INTO ACTION

"Nothing diminishes anxiety
faster than action."
– Walter Anderson

"Up to a point a man's life is shaped by his
environment, heredity, and changes in the
world about him; then there comes a time
when it lies within his grasp to shape the clay
of his life into the sort of thing he wishes it to
be... Everyone has it within his power to say,
'this I am today, that I shall be tomorrow.'"
– Louis L'Amour

"The purpose of life is to live it."
– Clarence Darrow

"Do the thing you think you cannot do."
– Eleanor Roosevelt

"Success is something you attract
by the person you become."
– Jim Rohn

Resilience is the ability to learn and grow from difficult events. It is a powerful character trait that I strongly recommend for anyone. In this third part, Getting Into Action, I propose two kinds of activities: ones that generate peace and joy as they promote more frequent "positive" or pleasant and supportive emotions; and ones that give you tools and tips to rebound when difficulty strikes. Together, they promote resilience.

Chapter 10

IT'S TIME!

"A goal without a plan is just a wish."
– Antoine de Saint-Exupéry

This is the time in the book when you start focusing on actions, routines, and specific healthy habits that can drive your happiness. The ideal plan, the plan optimized for YOU, can consist of a myriad of little things!

So far in the book, I have suggested that you try a variety of things to enhance your experience of reading the chapters. In this Part, I group all the activities that I want you to consider implementing.

Remember that these are activities so just reading about them will do NOTHING!

I encourage you to try them all and I have provided a Table in the Appendix where you can schedule each activity and also take notes after you have tried it. I do not expect you to incorporate all these activities into your life but trying them all will give you valuable information about what appeals to you versus what doesn't, what you feel compelled to improve in your life, and how the suggestions in this book can help you do exactly that.

Moreover, I encourage you to try several times; sometimes you can reap benefits from doing things even if they are uncomfortable at first. A good rule of thumb is to try a new activity seven times before deciding how you like it. The most recent research about habit forming says that you need to do something sixty-six times before it becomes habitual. So seven times is just to see how you like it.

Before going into the activities, it is useful to take some time to reflect on specifically what you are trying to achieve and what area(s) of focus spoke to you the most or sparked your interest.

It is very useful and some might even say indispensable to clarify your goals before you can chase them. If you found yourself drawn to the chapter on Your Physical Health, for example, it is useful to be more specific; indicating which section or area of physical health captured your interest. Perhaps you are having some issues with your sleep: not sleeping well or not sleeping enough. Perhaps there is something about the way you eat that is not agreeing with you. Perhaps it is on the exercise front that you wish to improve. Maybe it is your approach to healing that you are trying to figure out.

Maybe you don't have a particular health problem but you are interested in taking better care of your health nonetheless. In that case, you may be inspired to go further without a clearly defined pain point.

Do you lack information or do you not make the best choices? In other words, do you need to do research or do you need to work on your motivation?

I just walked you through possible focus points regarding your physical health. I now invite you to do the same for all the areas covered in Part II.

In Part II, Areas of Focus, I covered four broad topics.

1. In Chapter 6, I discussed your physical health and you reflected on your relationship with food, exercise, sleep and cultivating good health.

2. In Chapter 7, I discussed your emotional health. You did an exercise to notice how thinking about different situations generated different emotional

states. You also found your diaphragm and did a one-minute breath meditation.

3. In Chapter 8, you pondered your relationships and how connected you feel. You also thought about how you feel about your friendships and what you look for in a love relationship.

4. Finally, in Chapter 9, I approached spirituality and meaning. You pondered the quintessential "What for?" question and reflected on your purpose and meaningful causes. You focused on beauty and being in the present moment, thought about the link between living together and spirituality and you reflected on your relationship with money.

So you have already done a lot.

In this part of the book, you will take it to the next level. For each chapter from Part II, I invite you to ask yourself:

"How satisfied am I with where I am in this area of my life?"

You may want to take notes in your activity booklet or your notebook or you may prefer to loosely muse on this question. My aim here is to orient your attention in the chapters that follow, towards the activities that will be most beneficial to you.

How satisfied are you with:

- Your Physical Health?

- Your Emotional Health?

- Your Relationships?

- Your Spirituality and Sense of Meaning?

At the same time as I invite you to think about the areas of your life you wish to improve upon, I encourage you to approach each activity with an open mind.

In the next several chapters, I will describe a collection of routines and activities, and I invite you to make a note in Table 1 from the Appendix or in your activity booklet and plan when you will try them. This will launch the building of your personal plan of action.

Chapter 11

MORNING, EVENING, AND SLEEP

Routines have the advantage that they become exactly that: routines. When they become habitual, you have a good thing going! As long as you have picked them wisely, of course. While I focus on morning and evening routines, you may have routines at other times, and that is great too.

Morning Routines

A lot of people engage in some sort of morning routine. Some read, some write, some meditate, some go running or work out; there are many possibilities. It is important to find a routine that works for you and that suits your needs.

First you must ask yourself what you are aiming for in a morning routine. If you have trouble waking up, you might be aiming to wake up more completely. In that case, some form of physical activity might be a good idea in order to get your blood flowing. If you have trouble focusing in the morning, you might aim to control your focus and thoughts. In that case, you might want to focus yourself with meditation or visualization.

If you find that you have already committed to certain activities but you can't fit them into your busy schedule, your aim might be to complete that activity in the morning. In that case, you need to schedule time for that activity whether it be to read for half an hour, to write for some amount of time, or to exercise.

Personally, I like Hal Elrod's *Miracle Morning Routine* that covers all bases. You probably have heard of Hal's work but in case you haven't, let me summarize it here. The Miracle Morning Routine fits into the acronym SAVERS:

Silence (meditation)

Affirmations

Visualization

Exercise

Reading

Scribing (writing)

Hal gets up an hour earlier and does ten minutes of each of these activities. Personally, knowing myself, I am a night owl, and getting up a full hour earlier is too much for me but I have come to love my morning routine. I started with a much shorter version but my usual routine now takes about 45 minutes with transitions.

It goes like this:

Silence (meditation): 12 minutes

Affirmations: 2 minutes

Visualization: 4 minutes

Exercise: 6 minutes

Reading: 10 minutes

Scribing (journaling): 4 minutes

If I need to get up extra early, I try to do at least the first four steps and in a real crunch, I will do just the meditation. I am in my 7th year of doing some version of this morning routine and it really makes a big difference in my days.

Lisa Abramson and Vanessa Loder at "Mindfulness Based Achievement – the new MBA," include a morning routine in their success ritual. According to them, the way you start your day is essential to creating your success with ease.

In creating a morning routine, it is important to choose something that works for you; something that you feel both comfortable enough and satisfied enough with. Once you have picked something, try it for long enough to feel if it is having the effect you want. I recommend at least seven consecutive days.

I have been doing some version or another of The Miracle Morning for over 6 years, and I continue because I have experienced three major benefits:

1. I feel more awake and focused during the day, no matter whether I feel that I slept enough or not.

2. I have an easier time going to bed a bit earlier at night, which is a huge win for me as a night owl!

3. I am reading a 100-page monthly magazine that I find very interesting.

Activity #1: Take some time now to craft a morning routine that you would like to try.

Then try it. Then try it again. Try it seven days in a row to give yourself time to see how it is working for you.

Evening routines

Once again, it is important to identify what your needs are. Depending on whether you have trouble falling asleep or staying asleep, or you have trouble stopping with the day's activities to go to sleep, the recommendations won't be the same.

The purpose of an evening routine is obviously to put yourself in the best possible conditions for having a peaceful night of sleep. If you are a parent, you probably have experienced creating nighttime routines with your child(ren), whether it is a bath before bed, telling a story, listening to some music, or some other combination.

Let's start with the decision to go to bed. Some people can just pick up and go to bed in a few minutes whenever they feel tired in the evening. I used to be married to such a person. It always bewildered me.

Personally, I need time to transition, check that everything is alright, feed the cat, and prepare a few things for the next morning. And then I have my bathroom routine, cleaning my face, applying my night cream, etc. The whole thing can take up to an hour. You might be somewhere in the middle.

Whatever your style and rhythm in the evening, it is crucial to know how much sleep is enough for you and plan your evening routine accordingly. Say you get up at 7:00 and need 8 hours of sleep; you then need to turn off your light at 11:00 PM and therefore need to stop what you are doing in the evening with enough time to complete your routine before bed.

This may seem super trivial to you, and it does to me too. Except this is my single biggest tripping point in life. If you are a morning person, you might be thinking I am defective or something. If you are a night person, you can probably relate to this.

Night owls wake up in the evening and the urge to go to sleep just doesn't come until the wee hours of the night, so it takes real intention, and oftentimes it goes against the energy of the moment. It often does not feel like bedtime at the appointed hour needed to feel rested.

So, the night people will have an extra challenge compared with the morning people, and a nighttime routine may serve a purpose there. Here are a few ingredients of a nighttime routine; you should feel free to add your own:

- Have a soothing herbal tea, such as chamomile

- Light some candles

- Play some soft music

- Write down three things that went well for you today

- Write down one to three goals for tomorrow

- Take some time to read in bed if it helps you find sleep

- Take some time to journal

Activity #2: Take some time now to craft a nighttime routine that you would like to try.

Then try it. Then try it again. As I keep telling you, I recommend that you give yourself a full seven days before deciding if you like it or not!

Sleeping habits

Sleep is essential for your best possible self to have a chance of showing up. As I presented in Chapter 6, not getting enough sleep has all sorts of consequences, not the least of which is being in denial about how sleep-deprivation is affecting you. I recommend two activities for this topic. The first is a diagnostic.

Activity #3:

1. Go to bed 30 minutes earlier tonight than you usually do.

2. Don't change your alarm.

3. Notice if you wake up before your alarm.

   a. If you do, you have found your night length.

   b. If not, go to bed 30 more minutes earlier tomorrow night.

   c. Repeat until you wake up before your alarm.

4. Take stock of your sleep needs.

From this first activity, you will have a better idea of how much sleep your body requires for optimal functioning. You might try this several days in a row as there are, of course, days when you are more tired than other days.

The second activity is a stress-reducing one. Stress can mess with your sleep like nothing else! One way to relax, in general and for sleeping in particular, is to find your diaphragm. The Greeks call it the center of all expression. It is the key to how you regulate your system.

You already found your diaphragm in Chapter 7. If you need a reminder, put your thumb ½ an inch to an inch below your real or imaginary bra strap. That is your diaphragm. Now press lightly down with your thumb. As you breathe in, push your thumb away with your in-breath, and as you breathe out, your thumb should come back down.

Activity #4: Take three or four slow full breaths, in and out, as I just described. The diaphragm goes around so if you put your hands on your rib cage, you can feel the ribcage open as you breathe in and close as you breathe out.

What difference do *you* feel after doing this? Make a note of how it has affected you. It is a very easy, very portable, very accessible tool for stress-reduction, which may help you find your sleep.

Chapter 12

EXERCISE

Before starting on any new exercise routine, I strongly recommend that you see a doctor. It is probably okay, however, for everyone to walk more.

The next set of practices concern exercising. Again, there are some formal practices and some informal practices. Since I have been working out in a gym with a professional coach, for about an hour, three times a week, most weeks, for over 25 years, I have learned a few things about exercise.

I have a fairly high level workout regimen for a non-professional and I can tell you that getting my body to work, and to work hard sometimes, has yielded diverse benefits in terms of emotion regulation, quality of sleep, and physical abilities in my day-to-day life; thus, I view exercise as the cornerstone of my equilibrium.

What can exercise do for you? You will not know that until you try!

For exercise, just like for meditation, in order to get the most benefit, it is necessary to have a regular formal practice. How you do that and what you start with depends on your current exercise level.

If you have trouble motivating yourself to exercise, it is amazing how much easier that becomes if you find someone to do it with you. The accountability to another person is a very strong motivator.

If you are completely sedentary, you could start with walking for five minutes three times a week. After you do that for a few weeks, you can increase to 10 and then 15 minutes three times a week.

Or you might sign up for and go to a yoga class. You may have noticed that signing up for the class, just like reading this book, has no impact if you don't get into action. So find someone who has a similar goal and put on your walking shoes!

If you are already somewhat physically active, and you want to increase your level of fitness because it is good for your health, the possibilities are endless. Find something that you enjoy doing; it makes it more likely that you will follow through. Which activity will work for you will depend to a large extent on your ability to self-motivate.

You may join a gym and either attend classes or get a trainer who will take your specific goals into account and build a program for and with you. There are also a number of video-based programs available on the internet. Some programs use weights, some programs use bodyweight. There are two things to check for any program you are considering starting:

1. Is the advice you are getting sound? In other words can the source of the advice be trusted?

2. Are you motivated enough that you will follow through?

If you have answered YES to both these questions, you are good to go!

If the advice is not sound, find better advice. There is no shortage of offerings of exercise-related activities. If you do not feel motivated enough to follow through, then I send you back to Part I of the book to work on your mindset.

Let me remind you that exercising, among other things, will help you to have more willpower for other goals. This may be a sufficient motivator for some of you.

I may have a somewhat unusual ability to self-motivate, but I can tell you that I don't ever ask myself if I feel like working out. I schedule it, and I go when it is time to go. That became automatic after I really became aware of the benefits I was getting from my workouts.

For health reasons and for sustaining your willpower, it is desirable to have a formal exercise practice. Such a practice can be complemented, however, by more informal exercises. This is the exercise that you get in your day to day life.

Today, the World Health Organization (WHO), the US Centers for Disease Control and Prevention, the US Surgeon General, the American Heart Association, the US Department of Health & Human Services, and the National Heart Foundation of Australia all recommend that individuals take 10,000 steps a day to improve their health and reduce the risk of disease. Yup, that's right, ten thousand.

This will not happen without putting some intention behind it. You could park far away in the parking lot every time you park, and/or walk or bike instead of driving short distances. Another biggie is using the stairs. There are several reasons to use the stairs. Elevators actually use a lot of electricity to go up and down all day. So by using the stairs, you will get beneficial exercise AND save energy.

Exercise is beneficial for your health. You already know that. If you are currently not exercising or not exercising enough, you may need more than just me telling you to go exercise. In Chapter 19, you will learn five tips for forming new habits. In this chapter, I have laid out for you some known aspects of exercise and discussed my relationship to those aspects. As I do throughout this book, I urge you to figure out if and why you might want to modify your relationship to exercise, and then find an exercise routine that works for your preferences, for your schedule, and for your current body.

Activity #5: Decide on two plans of action that will improve your relationship to exercise.

Examples are:

1. Find a buddy and schedule three walks next week with them.

2. Sign-up for a gym and make an appointment with the trainer there.

3. Decide to walk for five or ten minutes at lunch time and put a reminder on your phone.

4. Join a local sports group in your area for a double benefit: increasing your exercise and having more human connection.

What are your plans of action? Decide this right now and then write in Table 1 when you will take your chosen actions.

Chapter 13

FOOD

I include this chapter on food because of the impact of healthy eating on willpower, our precious ally for reaching our goals. So in this chapter, you will find my recommendations for healthy eating, which I gathered during my own quest from sources I trust. Some of those sources are in the Sources of Inspiration section at the end of the book.

A common issue with food choices is motivation. A lot of people know better and yet consume a diet full of nasty stuff. If you recognize yourself in this description, you probably need to spend some time thinking about *WHY* you might want to eat a healthier diet.

Is it so that you are better able to keep up with your kids? Is it so you can have a better time with your partner? Is it to enhance your will-power? Would it enable you do your job better? What is *your* "WHY" for wanting to be healthier?

If this is your stumbling block, I recommend that you grab your activity booklet or a pen and a paper and take ten minutes right now to clarify that. Start writing: "I want to get healthier because..." and see what comes next.

Perhaps, you find that you lack willpower. If that is the case, I can tell you again that sleeping enough, eating well, and exercising are key supporters of your willpower!

So I recommend you concentrate on those activities that benefit you and strengthen your willpower as a byproduct.

Eat organic produce as much as possible.

This recommendation has two possible objections: availability of organic produce, and their price. Only you know where you stand regarding these objections.

In the case of financial issues, I would argue that by eating healthy foods, you may need to eat less of it for good nutrition and the benefit of this may offset the initial cost.

If you are interested in buying more organic produce, you might be interested in the following two lists. Dr

Weil and the Environmental Working Group have identified the produce with the highest and lowest pesticide residue.

The first list, the Dirty Dozen Plus (2021), contains the produce with the highest pesticide residue; thus, it is most important that you buy the organic versions of these items.

- Strawberries

- Spinach

- Kale/Collard/Mustard greens

- Nectarines

- Apples

- Grapes

- Cherries

- Peaches

- Pears

- Bell and hot peppers

- Celery

- Tomatoes

- Potatoes

By contrast, the Clean 15 list is comprised of the following fruits and vegetables, which have the <u>lowest pesticide residue</u>. You can buy these from conventional sources with less pesticide impact on your health.

- Avocados

- Sweet corn

- Pineapples

- Onions

- Papayas

- Sweet peas (frozen)

- Eggplant

- Asparagus

- Broccoli

- Cabbage

- Kiwifruit

- Cauliflower

- Mushrooms

- Honeydew

- Cantaloupe

Pesticides in your food can be detrimental to your health so it is preferable to avoid foods with high pesticide content. For foods with lower pesticide residue, it is still possible that large amounts of pesticides and herbicides are used on the farms from which these originate, contaminating groundwater, promoting erosion, and otherwise damaging local eco-systems.

So reducing the demand for chemical-heavy foods is a contribution to your health and beyond. To help promote the health of the planet as well as your own health, it's best to buy organic whenever you can.

Activity #6: Decide which foods you want to start buying organic.

Reduce sugar!

For health, environmental, and willpower reasons, it is recommended to massively reduce the sugar in your diet. I discussed this in Chapter 6 but in my honest opinion, it can bear to be repeated.

Sugar has recently been promoted to the rank of #1 enemy of our health. The list of diseases that become more likely as a result of consuming too much sugar is too depressing to include here. So if you are going to make only one change in your life to improve your quality of life, this would be my pick: reduce your sugar intake. Here are some suggestions:

a. Quit sugary drinks!

Nothing is quite as bad as drinking your sugar. First off, your body doesn't register the calories you drink as well as the ones you eat, so drinking sugar is a sure way to take in too many calories. Having sugar water in your mouth is also bad for your teeth. On top of that, consuming that much sugar in the first place is a really bad health choice.

Start replacing all your sugary drinks with water or unsweetened herbal teas. If you cannot wean yourself off of the sweet taste, it seems that Stevia and raw honey are some of the better options. Artificial sweeteners, while not as bad for your teeth, are not innocuous in your blood sugar regulation mechanism, according to medical sources and also Isabel de Los Rios, the founder of the Beyond Diet program. So still be careful of artificial sweeteners.

b. Quit industrial wheat-based products.

Industrial cakes, white bread and pasta, cookies, candy, etc., may include added sugar, but they also turn into sugar in your bloodstream very quickly. So-called whole wheat produced industrially is not much better, in terms of glycemic index. If you like bread, I recommend that you either make your own or find some that is made using artisanal methods with good quality ingredients.

c. Reduce hidden sugars.

A more advanced activity is to reduce your hidden sugar consumption. For this, you must look at the labels of the food you eat. A good rule of thumb is that if it ends in –ose, it is probably sugar, as in Sucrose, Maltose, and Dextrose, among others. Anything with syrup in the name is also likely to be a form of sugar.

One way to reduce hidden sugars is to eat natural foods.

Activity #7: Identify one to three sugar-related habits that you will change, for better health and willpower.

Adjust your meat consumption

Red meat has received a lot of negative attention for its environmental and health impact and also for the sometimes downright disgusting ways it is produced.

Back in 2008, the documentary *Food, Inc.* depicted some of the most shocking shenanigans of the food industry, concerning red meat among other practices. The alarming evidence on the negative health impacts of red meat is mitigated by other studies, but regardless, the idea of eating bleached hamburgers remains disgusting to me.

If you want to cut out meat altogether, it is important that you research what vitamins and minerals you will need to supplement.

My personal take on the issue is to eat less meat and to eat only high quality meat if you do eat it. I eat mostly free-range locally grown chickens and the occasional piece of pasture-raised beef; I seldom eat pork anymore.

I urge you to question your position on meat. What next step are you willing to take?

Activity #8: Do you wish to change your meat consumption? Take some time to ponder this. If you do, how will you do it?

Seasonings

When I describe some of my food choices, people often wonder about taste, as though eating less meat and more vegetables is synonymous with eating a bland diet. Not at all!

There are a myriad of seasonings. Pepper, ginger, turmeric, parsley, coriander, and mint, just to name a few, add flavor and health benefits for some. You can also add brewer's yeast for B vitamins and minerals.

The possibilities are endless. If you are looking for healthy yummy recipes, I recommend www.beyonddiet.com, which I have already mentioned. Check it out and be assured that I am not getting a commission.

Chapter 14

PRACTICES FOR A POSITIVE MINDSET

I recommend five practices for a positive mindset. They are Breathing into the Present Moment, Gratitude, Self-Compassion, Forgiveness, and Visualization – the Hindsight Window.

Breathing into the present moment

The first and most essential pillar for improving your mindset is to cultivate the ability to be present in the moment. The most direct and fool-proof way to do that is to spend some time every day focusing on your breath.

Start small, one minute when you wake up, and one minute before going to sleep. Increase gradually, see what you prefer. Maybe doing it in the morning gives you a better start to your day, and maybe doing it right before bed helps you settle for a good night's sleep.

If you have a long commute during which you are not driving, that might be a perfect time to develop a centering practice.

Practice this in the way that is most comfortable for you to fit into your daily routine, but practice it daily and you will see results.

Activity #9: Schedule one minute of focused breathing twice a day for seven days, and then do it! At the end of seven days, note how you like it.

Gratitude

The practice of gratitude has so many benefits that it is considered a meta-strategy for cultivating happiness and well-being. Having a practice of cultivating presence in the moment will help you get in touch with those things that bring positivity into your life and will facilitate the feeling of gratitude.

To incorporate the gratitude activity into your routine, I recommend that you start by doing it once a week, maybe Sunday evening. To practice gratitude, take some time to quietly reflect on the week that has elapsed. Let one to three pleasant things come to your mind. Write a short description of each event.

It really is more powerful to write it down rather than just think it; studies have shown that unequivocally. So you might want to get yourself a gratitude journal and have one page per week.

If you find that you enjoy it a lot, you can of course do it more often, but you want to avoid a situation in which it becomes an obligation and you start feeling like you have trouble coming up with three things to write about.

Emergency gratitude can be found in the realization that you have access to this present moment. If you are really stuck and cannot find a single thing to write about, I suggest the following:

"I am grateful for the present moment, for in it lies the possibility of the future I am creating."
– Sonia Weyers

Gratitude, or gratefulness, also comes in handy when you want to get out of "negative," unpleasant emotions. If you can muster the discipline to connect to something you feel grateful for in your life, you will find that your "negative" emotion is gone.

Activity #10: Next time you feel that an unpleasant emotion has a strong hold on you, look for something in your life you feel really grateful for and bring up the feeling of gratefulness.

Activity #11: Schedule 15 minutes in the next week to write about three things you are grateful for from the previous week. Be very specific in your descriptions and feel gratefulness blossom in your chest.

Forgiveness

Holding a grudge is a sure way to lower your sense of well-being. Perhaps you will have a sense of self-righteousness, but I don't think that will make you happy. Yet, forgiving can be difficult.

This activity is for you if you are feeling wronged in some way and you are having trouble letting go. It is based on the work of Fred Luskin from Stanford University.

Activity #12:

Start by thinking of a situation in which you feel wronged, you feel like someone has done you some harm that you are not able to forgive, to let go of. There are nine steps:

1. The first step is to become intimately familiar with how you feel about what happened. Do you feel sad? Do you feel angry? Do you think it was unfair?

    Try to clarify the way in which you feel wronged and the emotional impact it is having on you. Then you can tell a few trusted people about your experience.

2. Make a commitment to yourself to feel better. Remember that forgiveness is for you, to free yourself of these unpleasant feelings you are harboring.

3. Realize that forgiveness does not necessarily imply reconciliation with people who offended you nor does it mean condoning their actions; rather, your aim is to blame the offenders less and take their offenses less personally.

4. Become aware of what is happening: you are distressed over the hurt feelings and thoughts you are having at this time. You are not actually hurting from what happened then.

5. When the upset feelings are too much, it is important to soothe yourself. You can do the diaphragm exercise, do some deep breathing, and/or go into nature, whatever works best for you.

6. If you do not have the power to make something happen, it is best to give up expecting it. You might have been demanding something from the person who hurt you that they were not willing or able to give you. This causes suffering.

    Remind yourself that you can hope for and work hard for what you want, but you may not have the power to make it happen.

7. Focus on finding a way to get your positive goals met other than through the experience that has hurt you.

8. Realize that a life well-lived is your best revenge. If you focus on your wounded feelings, you give power to the person who has caused you pain. Instead of that, look for the beautiful things around you such as love, beauty and kindness.

    Put your energy into appreciating what you have rather than focusing on what you do not have.

9. Include your heroic choice to forgive in the way you look at your past.

When you have successfully forgiven someone who has hurt you, you will understand why it is so important. The weight lifted off your shoulders will help you enjoy life more and create more pleasant memories.

Self-compassion

This activity is a good one to pull out when you face a difficult situation, especially if you are used to beating yourself up when you don't measure up to your expectations! In that case, it may be difficult so start small. Maybe once a week is enough to start with.

This activity is composed of the three parts of self-compassion:

1. mindfulness
2. common humanity
3. self-kindness

In a moment when you are feeling difficult emotions, you may be tempted to tell yourself that you shouldn't be feeling this way. This is probably the most common, yet unproductive way to respond to a difficult emotion. Try picking a statement that reflects how you feel and say it to yourself: "This is a moment of suffering" or "this is hard" or "this hurts."

This is a way to mindfully connect with your emotional experience in the moment without judging it as either good or bad. The next step is to recognize an element of common humanity. Remind yourself of this common humanity by saying, "Suffering is part of life," or "Everyone struggles in their life."

The third and last step is to put your hands over your heart and try saying, "May I be kind to myself." In this way, you express self-kindness. Variations on the statement can include "May I give myself the support that I need" or "May I be strong in this moment."

Activity #13: Choose a phrase for each part of self-compassion: mindfulness, common humanity, and self-kindness. Use it next time you are falling short of your expectation. Notice how that feels.

A second self-compassion practice is the Metta meditation that you will find in Chapter 17 on spiritual practices.

Visualization – The Hindsight Window

The last activity for emotional health is visualization. The common way to visualize is to center yourself and then muse about the best possible outcome for some aspect of your life.

The visualization I propose to you for this activity is a bit different, and it is one of the most powerful techniques I have come across. Eric Edmeades talks about it beautifully: it is about shortening the Hindsight Window. Let me explain what this is.

You probably have somewhere in your memory, an event that was difficult, perhaps even downright tragic, and then, later in your life, a moment when you realized some good things happened as a result.

I can certainly credit my struggles in life for giving me the skills I have today for enhancing my life. Had I had a happier start in life, I would never have embarked on this quest, which is so satisfying today.

The hindsight window is the time between the difficult event and the time at which you can see the secondary benefit you have derived from that difficult event. It seems clear, from this perspective, that the shorter your hindsight window the happier you will be. Conversely, the longer your hindsight window the less happy you will be.

Activity #14:

1. Pick an event or situation that you are currently struggling with.

2. Ask yourself, "Why might I be grateful for this one day?"

3. Ask yourself again, "Why might I be grateful for this one day?"

4. Ask yourself yet again, "Why might I be grateful for this one day?"

5. When you begin to find answers to this question, you will have a new perspective on what is happening to you, and you will see that it will be OK.

So, in the words of Eric Edmeades, "The more gratitude you can have for your past, the more faith you can have for your future!"

Shrinking your hindsight window is a powerful way to get more happiness in your life and more gratitude for your past.

Chapter 15

SELF-CARE PRACTICES

For this chapter, I want you to start by reflecting on what makes you feel good in your life or what else you think would make you feel good. You are looking for concrete time-bound actions such as taking a warm bath, going for a walk outside, or curling up in bed with a good book.

These are practices that you can do for and by yourself. This is not to say you will suddenly become self-sufficient and not need anyone else. It is, however, a useful skill to be able to soothe and nurture yourself.

Activity #15: Find five self-care activities that appeal to you. Schedule them. Find an accountability partner and let them know what you are doing.

Let's detail each part of this activity.

Can you come up with five activities that will make you feel better if you do them? If you have trouble coming up with five, see if you can take inspiration from the following list.

- Take a warm bath

- Go for a run

- Go for a leisurely stroll in nature

- Sit in a comfortable chair and sip a warm beverage

- Read a book that interests you

- Listen to music you like

- Sit outside in the sun

- Light some candles and diffuse lavender essential oil in your bedroom and rest

- Whatever you can think of that will make you feel good without jeopardizing your future happiness

Do you have your five self-care actions? Now, I want you to take your calendar and schedule them all, with a minimum of one a week.

When you have done that, I want you to contact someone whom you feel comfortable talking to about the steps you are taking to improve your life. Tell them what you have scheduled and ask them if they would be willing to hold you accountable.

In addition, you may want to write your activities in your activity booklet or in Table 1 from the Appendix.

I will do:

1.

2.

3.

4.

5.

On: (date and time)

1.

2.

3.

4.

5.

Great! Now you have some self-care activities scheduled and accountability put into place. Feel free to expand on this chapter and keep adding new self-care activities to your weekly schedule.

Chapter 16

SOCIAL LIFE

There are two activities in this chapter. The first one is an activity for seeing people. The second one is planning and executing acts of kindness.

For the first activity, you will organize and plan outings to see people. There are a couple of simple steps to do this. First, I propose that you consider three broad categories of people to see: friends, family, and social groups.

Friends and family speak for themselves and by "social groups," I mean any collective setting you may be part of. Maybe you attend an exercise class, maybe you are part of a walking group, or maybe you sing in a choir.

Second, I invite you now to select one member of each category: one friend, one relative or group of relatives, and one specific social group. If you do not have a collective setting at this time, I invite you to think of one that you would like to try.

Third, for each of these people or settings, select a time and place and activity that you will schedule. You may want to coordinate with them, of course, and when you have done that, record your plan in your activity booklet.

As a result of this activity, you will have scheduled three separate events. I am counting on you to now mark those on your calendar and actually follow through. The other part of the activity is then to mindfully enjoy these events that you have scheduled and after you complete each one, reflect on how it has improved your experience and take notes in Table 1 and your activity booklet or notebook.

Activity #16: Schedule one activity with one member of each of the three categories: Friends, Family, and Social groups.

Friends:

Who? _____

Where? _____

What? _____

When? _____

Family:

Who? _____

Where? _____

What? _____

When? _____

Social group:

Who? _____

Where? _____

What? _____

When? _____

My hope for you is that once you have taken action on each of these plans, you will have a better sense of how your social life impacts your experience of life.

The next activity is very simple and very effective; it is to do something generous. There are several studies backing up the idea that generosity breeds happiness. I suggest that you try it out!

Activity #17: Schedule a generous act, do it and feel the impact.

Chapter 17

SPIRITUAL PRACTICES

In this chapter, I suggest four spiritual practices that are not linked to religious activity. If you practice a religion, you may already have your spiritual practices as part of that, but even so, you may be interested in trying these: Meditation, Connecting with Nature, Loving Kindness Meditation, and Visualization.

Meditation

There are several approaches to meditation. The one I am most familiar with is the type learned in Mindfulness Based Stress Reduction (MBSR) programs. As I discussed at length earlier in this book, the practice of mindfulness involves focusing one's attention on something, oftentimes the breath or physical sensations, without judgment.

In the last couple of decades, mindfulness has gone from being an esoteric practice for the select few to being in every self-help publication, online or offline; it appears in every health and well-being recommendation; it has even entered into the business world with its touted benefits on productivity.

It seems only a slight exaggeration to say that the ambient message is: to practice mindfulness assures you a great life and to not practice it... well do it at your own risk. I find it difficult to position myself in relation to such binary messages, and yet, I can truthfully say that taking the flagship 8-week MBSR class has had a profound impact on my life.

I just mentioned the MBSR curriculum, but what seems to me to be essential for finding the key to our empowered life is to have some sort of contemplative practice; a practice that quiets down our mind so that a more intuitive, wise, and deep part of ourselves can better be heard.

There are many types of contemplative practices, and if you either have experience with such a practice or feel attracted to another practice, I strongly encourage you to follow your heart. I found mindfulness, and it is working for me. I urge you to find something that works for you.

An MBSR teacher and practitioner, Dave Potter, has a website on which he offers the MBSR training for free. Doing it on the internet is, of course, not the same as doing it in a live group, but it can be a good way to get a flavor of the practice.

Whatever the practice you choose, there are two basic ways to practice. One is the formal practice and the other is the informal practice. A formal practice would be to sit quietly for some amount of time, every day, at similar times: for example, you could do it as part of your morning or evening routine. You can sit and focus on your breath, you can do a body scan, or you can listen to guided meditations. The common aspect of all these is that you devote time to the practice.

And then there is the informal part of the practice, which can be both a consequence and a reinforcing aspect of the formal practice. This can be called mindful living.

When you are stuck in traffic and you start getting annoyed, you might catch yourself, take a mindful breath, and then become more aware of your reaction. When you are doing dishes or standing in line, you might take the opportunity to scan your body for unnecessary tensions or become aware of unproductive thoughts that are racing through your mind. When you go tuck your child in at the end of a long exhausting and stressful day, you might think to center yourself first by taking three deeps breaths, for example.

The informal practice is the flower that blooms from the previous season's growth of the formal practice. It is not likely that you will be able to shift your attitudes in the flow of your daily life if you don't make some personal investment in some formal practice first.

Activity #18: Experiment with a formal contemplative practice.

Pick a formal practice that works for you. I recommend that you make this a part of either your morning or your evening routine. At the moment, I start my morning routine with my formal practice of breath meditation, affirmations, and visualization for fifteen to twenty minutes.

All these small ways of becoming more present throughout your day will have, I promise you, a positive impact on your experience of your life and on your relationships.

Connecting with Nature

The second spiritual activity is "Connecting with Nature." What I mean by this is to have an experience with nature. This can be as simple as gardening, watering your flower pots or planting something in one. It can also be as grand as contemplating mountains, the sea, the woods, large rural areas, or the sky, and feeling that you are connected to something bigger than yourself.

For maximum effect, I encourage you to find some nature, to breathe it in, and to think about how it all came about, how it happened that you can look at this scene. It may take some practice, but my hope for you is that you begin to have an experience of being one with nature, and the feeling of inner peace that comes with that.

Activity #19: Breathe in some nature and reflect on how it all came about. Notice how you feel.

Visualization

The third practice I suggest to you is a Visualization. You can lie down in a comfortable position, close your eyes, and begin to visualize a world compatible with your spiritual values. You may want to visualize a world in peace, a world of tolerance, a world of respect, and just let your mind show you what that would look like to you.

If you prefer to write, you can set a timer and write for 15 minutes, describing this world in as much detail as possible.

Activity #20: Set aside 15 minutes, make yourself comfortable in a quiet place, and visualize your ideal world. Notice how you feel afterwards.

This is an opportunity to live, in your imagination, in the world such as you wish for it to be. Our reptilian brains don't differentiate between imagination and reality, so you can give yourself an experience of living in your ideal world through your imagination.

Enjoy your voyage!

Loving Kindness Meditation

The fourth and last spiritual practice I suggest is a Loving Kindness Meditation, also called Metta. In this meditation, you repeat specific words and phrases that evoke a boundless warmhearted feeling.

To practice this, find a peaceful place and sit in a comfortable and relaxed position. You may want to start by taking a couple of deep breaths. You will start by directing the well-wishes towards yourself. As you say the phrases, allow yourself to feel the intentions they express.

Activity #21: Practice the Metta meditation described here.

Metta meditation

May I be safe and protected,
May I be happy and peaceful,
May I be healthy and strong,
May I live with ease, and
May I be held in loving-kindness

After directing the loving-kindness to yourself, bring to mind someone whom you feel warmly towards and direct the well-wishes to them. It may be easier if you bring up an image of them in your mind's eye.

May you be safe and protected,
May you be happy and peaceful,
May you be healthy and strong,
May you live with ease, and
May you be held in loving-kindness.

As you continue with this meditation, you will direct the well-wishes to other people.

Next you will direct them to someone you feel neutral towards, maybe someone you barely know.

After that, direct them to someone you have difficulty with.

When you send loving-kindness to someone you have difficulty with, you may experience some opposite feelings such as anger, grief, or sadness. Don't worry about this and try not to judge yourself for having these feelings. See if you can observe those feelings and continue the meditation anyway.

If it is too difficult, maybe try with someone whom you have less difficulty with. The practice is aimed to cultivate feelings of loving-kindness in your own heart and, with practice, you can then wish good things upon even those who have harmed you in some way.

You end the meditation by sending loving kindness to all living beings:

May we all be safe and protected,
May we all be happy and peaceful,
May we all be healthy and strong,
May we all live with ease, and
May we all be held in loving-kindness.

This is one of my favorite meditations! How do *YOU* like it? I encourage you to take some notes in your activity booklet or your notebook to capture your feelings and reflections.

Chapter 18

YOUR NEW
GOALS AND HABITS

"We are what we repeatedly do.
Excellence, then, is not an act but a habit."
– Aristotle

Congratulations, you have considered 21 activities that can improve your happiness levels. This chapter presents the last two activities to lead you to build a master plan with specific healthy habits that can drive your happiness.

It is time to look through your notes and decide on the new habits you want to incorporate into your life. Looking back to the four areas of focus, Your Physical Health (Chapter 6), Your Emotional Health (Chapter 7),

Relationships (Chapter 8) and Spirituality and Meaning (Chapter 9), I invite you to choose one goal for each area. For example, for your emotional health, goals could be:

-    I want to feel less stressed

or

-    I want to be less reactive

or

-    I want to feel more positive emotions

Take time now to prioritize one goal for each of the four areas of focus. You can write down your goals in your activity booklet. If you feel completely satisfied with one of the areas, you can leave that area blank, but I encourage you to wonder if things couldn't be even better.

Activity #22: Define your priority goals.

For my physical health, my top goal is:

For my emotional health, my top goal is:

For my relationships, my top goal is:

Regarding spirituality and meaning, my top goal is:

You should now have anywhere between 0 (not so likely given that you have read this book to this point) and four goals you are interested in pursuing. Next, you will choose some actions that will move you closer to your goals.

But first, let us go over some considerations about getting into routines and creating habits.

Getting into routines

Part I of this book on mindset and attitude showed you how to best ensure that you will follow through with the actions YOU decide to take. To further help you implement the needed changes, you should take note of how actions become habits.

A lot of claims have been made about how long it takes to create a habit. Twenty-one days has been thrown around a lot. Yet, the latest research from University College London, says it takes 66 days <u>on average</u> to make a new behavior habitual. The truth is that it really depends on people and activities. Here are things that can help you succeed in creating new habits.

1. If you have identified <u>WHY</u> you want to change a habit or create a new one, and if that WHY is sufficiently important to you, you will have a much easier time drumming up motivation. *I want to do this because I read an article that said it was a good idea* is unlikely to provide much of any motivation. ***I want to do this because it will improve my quality of life for the long run*** is much more likely to work. So <u>pick habits that you can justify to yourself</u>.

2. Tie the new habit to an existing habit. Christine Carter discusses this tactic in her free webinars on creating habits that stick.

For example, if your goal is to floss more, but you already brush your teeth, then you would do well to piggy back your new flossing habit to your pre-existing teeth brushing habit.

When you pick a new activity that you wish to start, see if you can identify an activity you already do and make your new objective to add the new behavior to the existing habit.

3. Defensive pessimism. Think about the various ways in which you could get derailed and plan how you will get back on track. You can go back to Chapter 2 if you need a reminder of the detailed steps for defensive pessimism.

4. Get a buddy. It helps a lot to have someone who will help you on the path to accountability, and you might be able to return the favor by helping them to change some of their behaviors and improve their life.

5. Circle back to motivation. If you feel that summoning the needed motivation is your biggest challenge, I encourage you to start with one behavioral change at first and know that you can always go back to Part I for your shot of motivation.

Creating healthy habits has one wonderful benefit: you won't need so much willpower that way; your habits will just kick in!

Activity #23: Create your Action Plan.

Using your notes from your activity booklet or your notebook and from Table 1, ask yourself the following two questions for each activity:

1. Did this activity make me feel more peace, meaning or joy?

2. How can this activity contribute to my goals?

Let the answers to these two questions guide you to select up to three activities per goal. You can write down your plan in your activity booklet, in your notebook or you could type it up and frame it somewhere prominent, whatever you think makes it most likely that you will follow through with it.

GOAL I:

  – Action 1:

  – Action 2:

  – Action 3:

GOAL II:

    – Action 1:

    – Action 2:

    – Action 3:

GOAL III:

    – Action 1:

    – Action 2:

    – Action 3:

GOAL IV:

    – Action 1:

    – Action 2:

    – Action 3:

This ends the "Getting into Action" part. I hope you were able to find activities that resonate with you and that you will follow through on the plan you have just created.

If you haven't already, I encourage you to join our Facebook Group:

"Happiness Now! A Guided Journey."

CONCLUSION

Congratulations, you have reached the end of this book. I hope you feel motivated to bring change into your life. Before I send you off to the next greater version of you, let's sum up what you have learned.

In Part I, you learned the ingredients of motivation. In Part II, you discovered important areas of focus: Your Physical Health, Your Emotional Health, Your Relationships, Your Spirituality and Meaning. In Part III, you chose among 23 different activities those you want to incorporate into your life starting RIGHT NOW!

It is only through action that you will really discover new experiences and change. In this book, I have given you the very best information and actions to take your experience of life to the next level.

More broadly, I encourage you to seek new experiences as much as you can. It is through experience that you learn holistically, through body, mind, and soul.

On your way to a better life, remember to use the following set of questions to stay true to yourself. They will help you to seek experiences that are meaningful for you.

- Where? Where are you starting from, what are your beliefs about your situation? Are these beliefs serving you or can you improve on them?

- What? What are you trying to achieve, have you visualized your desired outcome? Be clear and specific about your vision.

- Why? What is your purpose in trying to achieve this? Your purpose is what drives you and this is probably the most important thing to consider.

- How? And finally, how are you going to go about achieving this goal, what are the steps, what is your strategy?

I hope you have found some answers in this book and that you have indeed found greater peace, meaning and joy. I wish you all the best in your search for a better life!

Writing this book was a new experience for me, and I learned a tremendous amount about myself in the process. I would not have written it without a reader like you in mind. Please stay in touch in the Facebook group "Happiness Now! A Guided Journey."

Thank you!

URGENT PLEA

Thank you for reading my book!

I really appreciate all of your feedback, and I love hearing what you have to say. I need your input to make the next version of this book better, as well as any other book I may write. Please take two minutes now to leave a helpful REVIEW on Amazon, letting me know what you thought of the book:

https://amazon.com/review/create-review?&asin=2956107917

Thank you so much!

Sonia Weyers
Your Happiness Guide
Founder of Eudokima
https://eudokima.com/en/

ACKNOWLEDGEMENTS

Private circle:

First and foremost, I thank my parents: you brought me into this world and launched me on this path of continuous self-discovery. I know that you have supported me every step of the way to the best of your abilities.

Next, I thank the father of my children: not only did you always support my changing goals, you have given me my dream of having four children, and I thank you for that; they are my primary source of inspiration.

Last but not least, I thank my partner and lover: your love and appreciation have been the greatest driver of my growth for the last decade; if not for you, I might still be stuck in the claws of unhappiness. From the bottom of my heart, thank you.

Larger circle:

For supporting me during the sometimes agitated moods I experienced during the book process, thank you to Valérie, Laura, and Natacha.

For the amazing experience at Self-Publishing School:

- Thank you, Chandler Bolt and Sean Sumner, and all the supporting team for running such an amazing process;

- thank you, Scott Allan and Kerk Murray, for your friendly and supportive guidance;

- thank you to the mastermind community for the qualiy of your responses;

- and most of all thank you, Corinne Tanguy, for being the best accountabilibuddy, for the first version of this book!

For reading an earlier draft and contributing to this version of the book, I thank Dawn Jarish, Vanessa Jolet, Robin de Lafforest, Bento Leal, Bérangère Noyau, Kelly Robic, Marta Urbina, Esther van Weelden, Jacques Weyers, Esther Wojcicki, Clara Zemsky, Gabrielle Zemsky, and especially Kate Philips-Kaiser.

Moreover, I wish to thank Katie Chambers, whose amazing professional editing greatly improved my writing and Marcy Pusey for her final proofreading.

Last but not least, I thank Esther Wojcicki for writing such a well-documented foreword. I respect your opinions greatly and have for all those years. You are truly an inspiration.

SOURCES OF INSPIRATION

Isabel De Los Rios and Beyond Diet: Eating plans, recipes and healthy living programs.
www.beyonddiet.com

Sharecare platform: A RealAge test and resources to create a healthy life.
about.sharecare.com

Dr Andrew Weil: Comprehensive health advice
www.drweil.com

***

The Berkeley Greater Good Center: the science for a meaningful life.
greatergood.berkeley.edu

Science of Happiness Massive Open Online Courses:

- "The Science of Happiness"

   www.edx.org/course/science-happiness-uc-berkeleyx-gg101x-4

- "Positive Psychology"

  www.coursera.org/learn/positive-psychology

- "A life of Happiness and Fulfillment"

  www.isb.edu/a-life-of-happiness-and-fulfillment

Mindvalley Academy: Online personal development classes.
www.mindvalleyacademy.com/

- Eric Edmeades on the Hindsight Window

  www.youtube.com/watch?v=cD16oT4tqVs

Deepak Chopra and Oprah Winfrey Meditations:
chopracentermeditation.com

Christine Carter: A sociologist who writes about productivity, parenting, happiness and living your best life.
www.christinecarter.com

Hal Elrod : The Miracle Morning.
halelrod.com

Caroline Goyder at TedX Brixton: "The surprising secret to speaking with confidence."
https://www.youtube.com/watch?v=a2MR5XbJtXU

Mindfulness Based Achievement: MBA course and 30-day meditation challenges.
http://www.mindfulnessbasedachievement.com/

My Lifebook Online: an online course for creating your life.
mylifebook.com/yes-mylo1/

Ted Talks: https://www.ted.com/

- Robert Waldinger: On the Study of Adult Development at Harvard.

  https://www.ted.com/talks/robert_waldinger_what_makes_a_good_life_lessons_from_the_longest_study_on_happiness

- Elizabeth Gilbert : On success, failure, the drive to create and genius.

  o https://www.ted.com/talks/elizabeth_gilbert_success_failure_and_the_drive_to_keep_creating

  o https://www.ted.com/talks/elizabeth_gilbert_on_genius

Finally, I credit my trainings to become a therapist and coach and my experiences on both sides of these activities as sources of inspiration for this book.

APPENDICES

Appendix 1:

Here are the different
ways I can support you further.

Your free guide to follow along the activities I give you in the book

https://eudokima.com/happiness-now-guide

Your free Openness Meditation.

https://eudokima.com/openness-meditation

Your free guide "The 5 Things in the Way of Your TRUE Happiness"

https://eudokima.com/5-things

My TedX "Finding Happiness: How Forgiving My Mother Radically Changed My Life"

https://eudokima.com/tedx

To find out about the therapy services I offer, for individuals and couples

https://eudokima.com/therapy

To find out about my 1-year program, *The "Experience Your TRUE Happiness" Haven*

https://eudokima.com/the-haven

Appendix 2:

Table 1

	Activity :	When :	Observations
1	Morning Routine		
2	Evening Routine		
3	Sleep Needs		
4	Diaphragm Breaths		
5	Exercise Plans		
6	Organic Foods		
7	Sugar Reduction		
8	Meat Consumption		
9	Focused Breathing		
10	Gratitude as a tool		
11	Gratitude practice		

12	Self-compassion phrases		
13	Forgiveness		
14	Hindsight window		
15	Self-Care x 5		
16	Social life		
17	Generosity		
18	Contemplative practice		
19	Nature		
20	Visualization		
21	Metta meditation		
22	Priority goals		
23	Action plan		

SELF-PUBLISHING
SCHOOL

NOW IT'S YOUR TURN

Have you ever thought of writing a book?

I had never thought I would write a book, that was until I encountered Self-Publishing School. They helped me write my book and they can help you too, with a free resource to start outlining your own book!

Even if you're busy, bad at writing, or don't know where to start, you CAN write a bestseller, that's what I did!

Self-publishing school is the one-stop resource you need to take YOUR book to the finish line.

Say "YES" to telling you story!

https://self-publishingschool.com/friend/

Just follow the steps on the page to get the FREE resource that will get you started on your book and unlock a discount to get started with Self-Publishing School.

www.ingramcontent.com/pod-product-compliance
Lightning Source LLC
Chambersburg PA
CBHW061609120626
46550CB00004B/1657